MEREDITH CHRONICLES

MEREDITH CHRONICLES

Passing Time on Lake Winnipesaukee

DANIEL HEYDUK

THE History PRESS

Published by The History Press
Charleston, SC 29403
www.historypress.net

First published 2015

Manufactured in the United States

ISBN 978.1.62619.763.3

Library of Congress Control Number: 2014958079

To my wife, Beverly, for all of our life's adventures.

Contents

Acknowledgements

I owe many thanks to the people at the *Meredith News*, the Meredith Historical Society and the Meredith Public Library for their assistance and support while this long project was unfolding. My wife, Beverly, gave me timely encouragement and proofread the text. Many individuals helped me to locate sources and learn Meredith history, and each of their contributions was uniquely valuable. In that regard, I am very grateful for the help and support of:

Catherine Amidon
Erin Apostolos
Cristina Ashjian
Evelyn Auger
Melanie Benton
Richard Boisvert
Ann Butler
Freda Perkins Cronin
Dawn Dever
Judy Dever
Clint and Jean Dougan
John Edgar
Paul and Kristen Eldridge
Vikki Fogg
Judy Hodges

John Hodsdon
Herman Kimball
Christopher Leland
John Moulton
Rita Polhemus
Jane Rice
Janis Roberts
John Sherman
Bonnie Sousa
Steve Taylor
Beverly Wilson
Barbara Jones Woodward
Esther Wyatt

Introduction

Looking at Meredith's history, it is surprising how many times things have changed. The people of Meredith, New Hampshire, were constantly challenged to adapt to new circumstances, and sometimes they changed the circumstances themselves. To describe those changes, I found that I had to look into how things worked at different times in the past and into what was happening outside the town. The result is a book about Meredith and its times in which, hopefully, local things like land speculation, sheep-raising and children's camps are more than just the *where* and *when*. Why a piece of land changed hands many times before anyone did anything to it, why there were briefly more sheep than people and why Lake Winnipesaukee had more than thirty children's camps at one time were just a few of the questions I wanted to answer.

There were also moments in history I wanted to explore, like Dudley Leavitt teaching, writing and working his farm; John Swasey remaking Meredith Village's water power; Sol and Lizzy Lovejoy running an island hotel; or the town coming together to put on a winter carnival. I wanted to learn enough about these events to make them real again.

Readers of my column, "Passing Time," which appears in the *Meredith News*, will recognize some familiar titles and phrases, but much that appeared there has been rewritten, and much has been added. I learned a lot while researching and writing those columns, but what appeared in a column was seldom the last word, as I often found out more. Also, this book has allowed me to follow trends and patterns through longer periods of time and place them in a bigger picture.

The chapters are organized by subject, but there is also a natural chronological progression, thanks to Meredith history itself. During the time covered in this history, trends appeared, lasted a while and then gave way to something else. The chapters roughly follow and describe that sequence. I chose to stop at the point where living memory begins, the decade of the 1930s. Meredith has changed again since then with the disappearance of the mills and the growth of the hospitality industry, but this time within living memory would require a somewhat different approach.

Chapter 1

Ancient Beginnings

The first people in Meredith came not long after the rivers began to run and the lakes were formed. About fourteen thousand years ago, the mile-high glacier that had over-topped all of our mountains, carved our valleys and scoured out the basins of our lakes melted to reveal a barren land. The first plants to grow were tundra mosses, grasses and wildflowers, and these attracted herds of grazing animals: mammoths, musk oxen and caribou. Physically modern people were already in North America and had learned to follow and hunt these herds, carrying their belongings with them and setting up camps. On the bare slopes of the surrounding volcanic hills—the Ossipees, Belknaps and Red Hill—they found the preferred stone to make their spear points, knives, hide-scrapers and woodworking tools. Animal bones, antlers and wood provided material for other tools, and hides were made into clothing and tents. These were the Paleoindians, and the record of their time here—from about twelve thousand to ten thousand years ago—has been unearthed at various locations around New Hampshire and the Northeast.

One of the intriguing things about the Paleoindians is that they came into this territory at the height of a severe cold climate shift that lasted for more than one thousand years. During that time, glaciers re-advanced, trees retreated south and the climate remained cold and dry. The herds of grazers, and especially caribou, thrived under such conditions, and that may be what drew the hunters here. The land was open, so they could see their quarry from a distance. The lakes and large rivers were dependable water sources for both hunters and hunted, while many of today's small streams were dry due to the climate. The Paleoindians probably followed the herds along well-established migration routes, camping on the river terraces and lakeside slopes. In addition to meat from the animals they hunted with stone-tipped spears, there were arctic cranberries and blueberries in season, water lily roots from the shallow water and other foods to gather along the way. The bands of people were not large—probably just a few families—and they kept together for security. Also roaming the territory at that time were huge short-faced bears, dire wolves, sabre-tooth cats and lions. Less-threatening giant beavers and ground sloths lived here and may have been hunted.

Based on historically known caribou hunters living in similar environments in the Canadian arctic, we can envision camps of skin tents, with other frames raised above the ground for drying and storing food and hides. There would

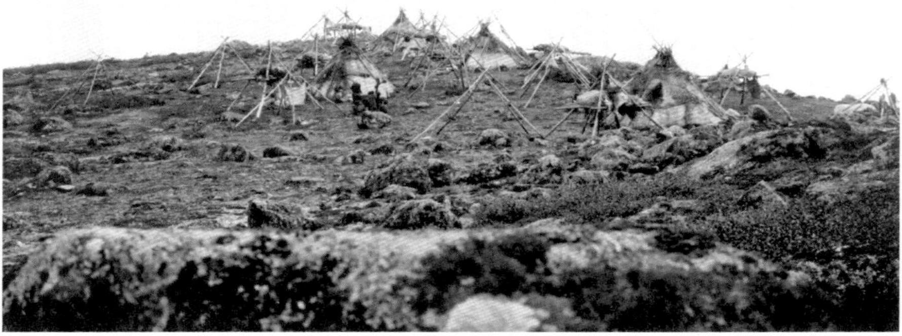

A caribou hunters' camp in northern Canada, 1910. *National Anthropological Archives, Smithsonian Institution (Cabot 1910.73, detail).*

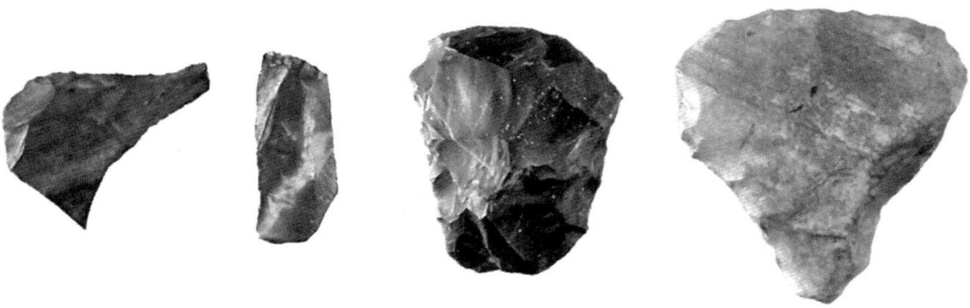

Small Paleoindian stone tools for working wood, antler, bone and hides. *Richard Boisvert.*

have been areas where tools were being made from rough stone "blanks" brought from quarries, probably using antler hammers to do the highly precise chipping. Wood was used for tent frames, spear shafts and "atlatls"—held in the hand and fit into the end of the spear for throwing with added force. Cooking was done over fires but without pottery, which had not been invented and would have been hard to carry, in any case.[1]

Many things changed when the climate warmed about ten thousand years ago. The tundra and "steppe" grassland environment was replaced by continuous forest, the grazing animals moved farther north and many became extinct, along with the large bears, wolves and cats that had preyed on them. The Paleoindian way of life ended, but people adapted with an "Archaic" forest and waterside lifestyle that lasted for thousands of years more.

The Archaic people lived in camps and settlements for weeks and months compared to the mere days that the Paleoindians had camped in a given spot. They took a variety of forest- and wetland-dwelling animals, birds, fish and shellfish—all the wild animals known to us today. They also used a greater variety of tools, indicating many different ways of getting food—hunting, trapping, fishing, taking wildfowl and gathering wild edibles. People were harvesting roots, wild plants, nuts and berries and processing them with mortars and pestles. They used ground-stone as well as chipped-stone tools. They also had things that came from far away via trade, visiting and seasonal get-togethers with other groups.[2]

From nine thousand to three thousand years ago, these early residents lived along lakes and rivers, camping at falls for fish migrations, settling at the lakeshore or the coast in summer and retreating to the deeper woods for winter. Stonedam Island, the Weirs and the Winnipesaukee and Waukewan lakeshores hold signs of their settlements. They lived in the same locations we favor today because the food resources of both land and water were available there. Those locations also were convenient for transportation and trade. People made dugout canoes by laboriously hollowing out tree trunks with stone tools and fire, but they could not easily carry these heavy boats around rapids or falls or overland from water to water.

At that time, one of the most useful inventions in this land of lakes, ponds, rivers and streams was the birch-bark canoe. Naturally waterproof birch bark was used for house coverings and for making containers, but its first use in canoes enabled much more wide-ranging travel than before. Birch-bark canoes gave access not only to lakes and rivers but also to narrow, winding streams and disconnected waters.

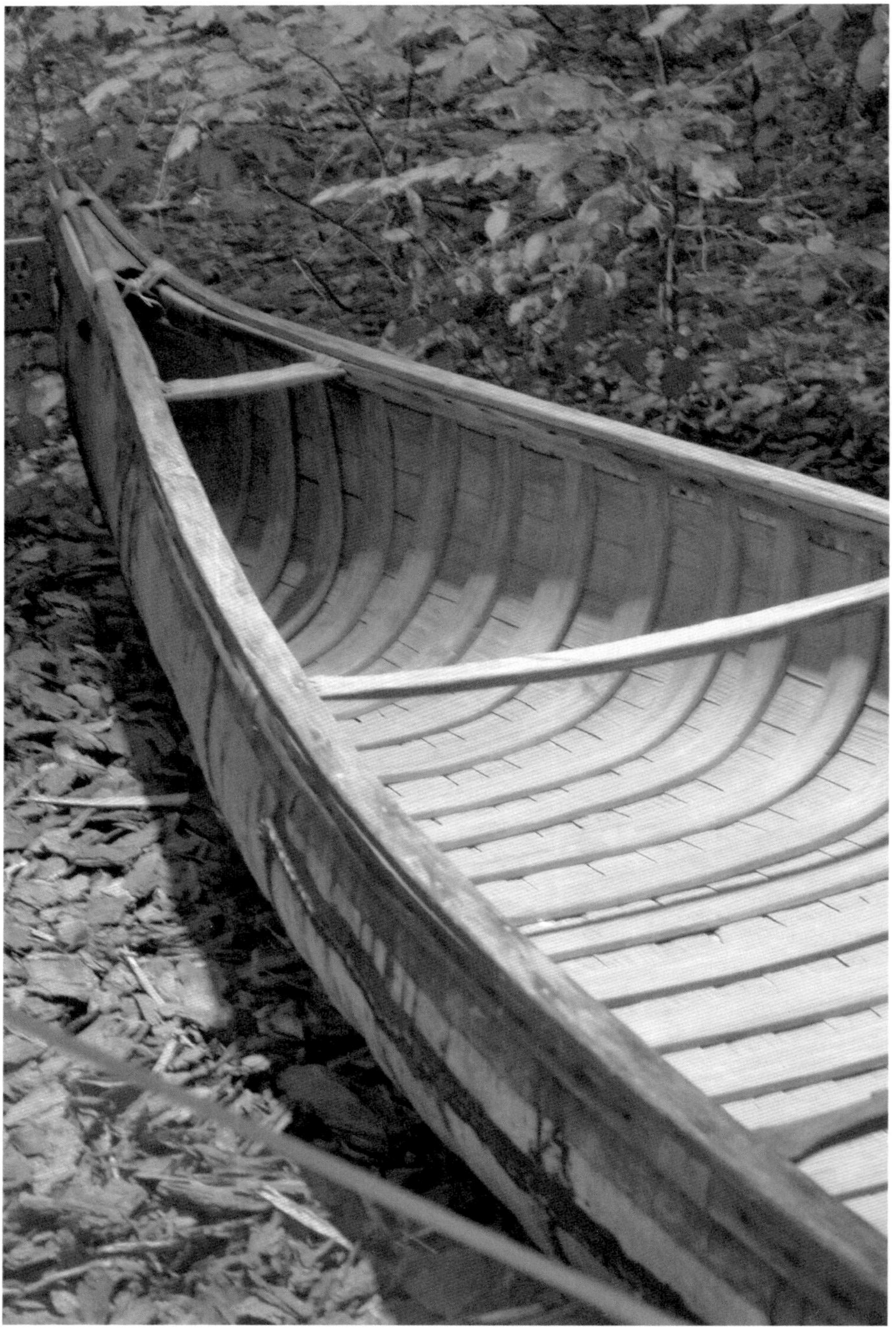

The birch-bark canoe revolutionized water travel. *Mount Kearsarge Indian Museum.*

The local forest provided everything necessary to build a canoe, and experts still build them today using simple tools. The bark of paper or canoe birch has grain that runs around the tree, allowing it to be cut and peeled in large rectangular sheets. The sheets were stitched together using the very long, flexible roots of black spruce, which grows in bogs and waterlogged soil. The sheathing and the curved ribs forming the inside of the canoe were made of spruce or northern white cedar, both of which are light, strong, easily split to a uniform thickness and flexible when steamed. Straight-splitting hardwood, such as ash or maple, was used for making thwarts and paddles. The rails, which run along the top of the canoe lengthwise, were made of cedar or spruce. After the bark was stitched together and attached to the rails by stitching and wrapping, spruce gum was used to seal the seams. Sheathing was then laid inside from bow to stern, and curved ribs were inserted from rail to rail to give the canoe its shape and stiffness.

Since all the materials are elastic, birch-bark canoes could be made in many different sizes and shapes to fit various uses. Unlike the dugout, the birch-bark canoe was strong but light, rode high in the water when empty, could be heavily loaded, be repaired anywhere in the forest and could easily be carried overland on the paddler's shoulders.[3]

In the Lakes Region, this canoe allowed Native Americans to move camp at will; fish; go up narrow, winding streams to hunt and trap; and travel long distance for trade and warfare. It put Meredith in a transportation network going west and south via the Winnipesaukee and Merrimack Rivers and north from Lake Winnipesaukee, via overland canoe "carries," to Lake Kanasatka, Wakondah Pond and Squam Lake. From Squam, paddlers could go east to Lake Ossipee via the Bearcamp River or west to the Pemigewasset River via the Squam River. One of the main water travel routes on Lake Winnipesaukee was east from the Weirs, past the southern point of Meredith Neck and then north along Center Harbor Bay to the overland carry to Lake Kanasatka.

Beginning about three thousand years ago, a time known as the "Woodland Period," people added bows and arrows, pottery and the growing of food to the local lifestyle. They continued to live in many of the same waterside locations, clearing fields nearby to grow corn, beans and squash. Lacking metal tools, Woodland people did not clear fields as the Europeans later would. Instead, they girdled or burned the bases of forest trees to kill them and then planted around the tree trunks in the soft lakeshore or river floodplain

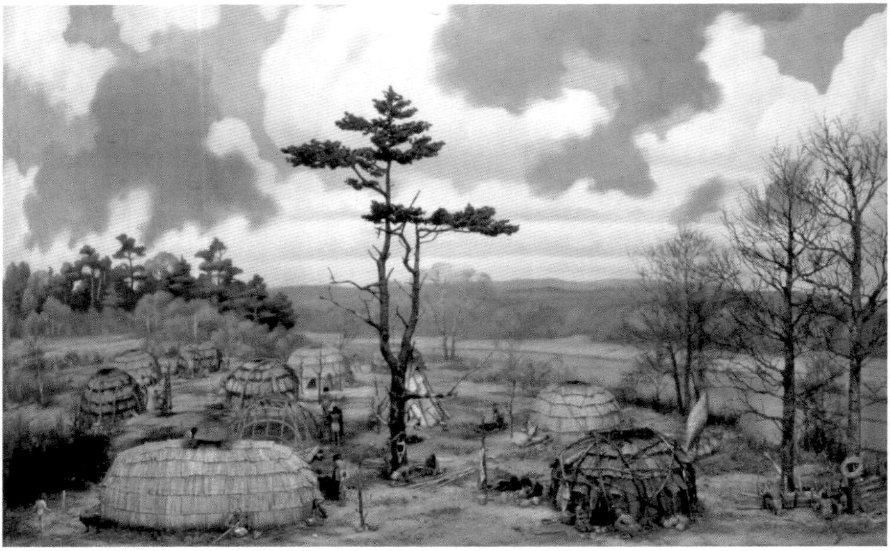

A Woodland Period waterside settlement. *Shattuck Farm Diorama, copyright Robert S. Peabody Museum of Archaeology, Phillips Academy, Andover, Massachusetts.*

soil that was exposed to the sun. After several years, fertility declined, a new patch of forest was prepared, and the old one returned to forest cover.

In this way, and by traditional hunting and gathering, the Woodland Native Americans used the Lakes Region land without changing it. They continued to visit shallow natural quarries to obtain the fine-grained, straight-fracturing stone they preferred for tool-making. They visited clay deposits, like that at the old Weirs Brickyard, to dig clay to make their ceramic pots. The Native Americans' stone tools were not good for felling large trees, so most of their woodworking was with smaller trees and with bark. Except for the stone tools and pottery fragments that they left behind, the things they made quickly disintegrated and the places where they lived returned to forest, with perhaps just a pile of shells or some charcoal from their cooking fires to mark the spot.

By the time Europeans arrived on the coast in the 1500s and New England history began to be recorded, Native Americans had been living here for more than ten thousand years. Europeans traded manufactured goods for the native people's corn and furs, and they enthusiastically adopted Native American canoes to travel the region's waterways. The Native Americans' way of life changed with European contact. European demand for furs, especially for beaver pelts, led to over-trapping and to the eventual extirpation of beaver in the Lakes Region. As the beaver disappeared, so the many ponds they had created dried up into meadows, and many other species—mammals, birds, fish, reptiles, amphibians and insects—that depended on the ponds for sustenance and reproduction were reduced.

Tragically, the Europeans also introduced diseases such as smallpox, measles, whooping cough, influenza, typhus, typhoid and plague, for which the native people had no resistance. Successive epidemics over several generations reduced the native population of New England by up to 90 percent. Many settlement sites that had been used for thousands of years were abandoned as the surviving people gathered together in just a few locations. Forest reclaimed the former settlements, so that there was little evidence that anyone had ever lived there.[1]

Chapter 2

The Empty Land and the New Town

Before 1600, settlements of Abenaki Native Americans were numerous, at the Weirs, Stonedam Island, Meredith Village, Center Harbor, Holderness Village and many other locations favorable for water access and horticulture. European diseases killed many of the Abenakis, reducing them to just a few towns. While the Lakes Region became largely empty of people, on-and-off hostilities between the French and their Native American allies to the north and the British colonies to the south kept the area from being settled by either side.

After King Philip's War between several New England tribes and the British colonies in 1675–76, the Abenakis withdrew to the north. Their last settlement at Aquadoctan (the Weirs) was abandoned in 1696. During continuing British-French hostilities in the 1700s, the Pemigewasset and Merrimack Rivers were followed by raiders from Canada who attacked towns all the way to northern Massachusetts, carrying off captives. Dover, Durham and the New Hampshire coast were repeatedly attacked via Lake Winnipesaukee and the Cocheco River, while York, Maine, was attacked via the Saco. Military expeditions were organized from those towns to pursue or intercept the raiders and destroy their camps. Both sides took scalps during these hostilities and were paid government bounties for them. Captain John Lovewell of Dunstable, Massachusetts, led two expeditions in the winter of 1724–25 to Lake Winnipesaukee, the Bearcamp valley and Lake Ossipee, attacking and killing Abenakis he met at Winnipesaukee and at Lovewell Pond. His third expedition via

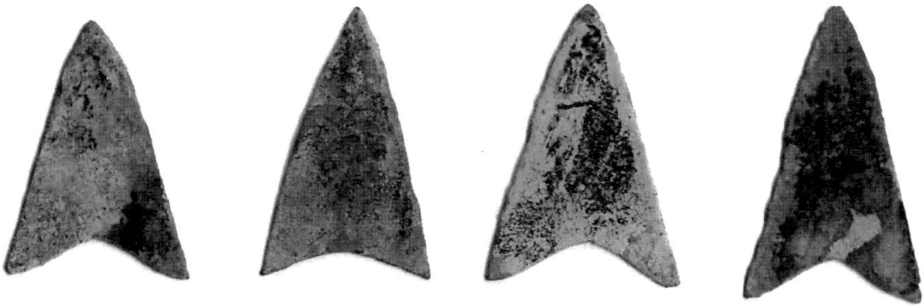

Native American arrowheads made from European trade brass. *Richard Boisvert.*

Winnipesaukee to Lake Ossipee in the spring of 1725 resulted in a pitched battle in which Lovewell and eleven of his men, as well as Abenaki chief Paugus and an unknown number on his side, were killed.[5]

France and England signed a treaty, and a period of twenty years of relative quiet followed during which colonial settlement pushed north to Canterbury and some Abenakis returned to the upper Pemigewasset. An Abenaki named Coaus visited Portsmouth in 1743 to ask Governor Wentworth that a trading post be established somewhere convenient to the river. He said that at least fifteen Abenakis would trade furs there. Wentworth chose Canterbury, and the assembly voted funds for rum, blankets, cloth for stockings, shirt linen, powder, shot, bullets and flints, pipes and tobacco to stock a trading post. Hostilities between the French and British began again in 1744, known as the French and Indian War, so Canterbury settlers built a blockhouse, and a permanent militia garrison was stationed there.[6] That became the hostile frontier, and neither the colonists nor the Abenakis thought about moving into the now unpopulated Lakes Region. To provide protection, a regiment under Colonel Theodore Atkinson was sent to the vicinity of Silver Lake (now Tilton) in 1746–47. The group built a fort and spent much time exploring the lakes, hunting and fishing. From this visit, the attractions and resources of the region became more widely known.

In 1748, the "Masonian Proprietors" held title by royal grant to a big piece of the colonial Province of New Hampshire, including all the land around Lakes Winnipesaukee and Winnisquam. They were granting new towns in this territory, and one of the towns created that year was Palmerstown, later called Salem and New Salem, and incorporated in 1768 as "Meredith." Acquiring the grant were eighty men from Hampton, Stratham, Exeter and Nottingham who committed themselves to settle the new town. First, however, the untracked, forest-covered land had to be surveyed into lots. Surveyors were hired to enter the no-man's land of the Lakes Region during the hostilities of the French and Indian War.[7] At times between 1749 and

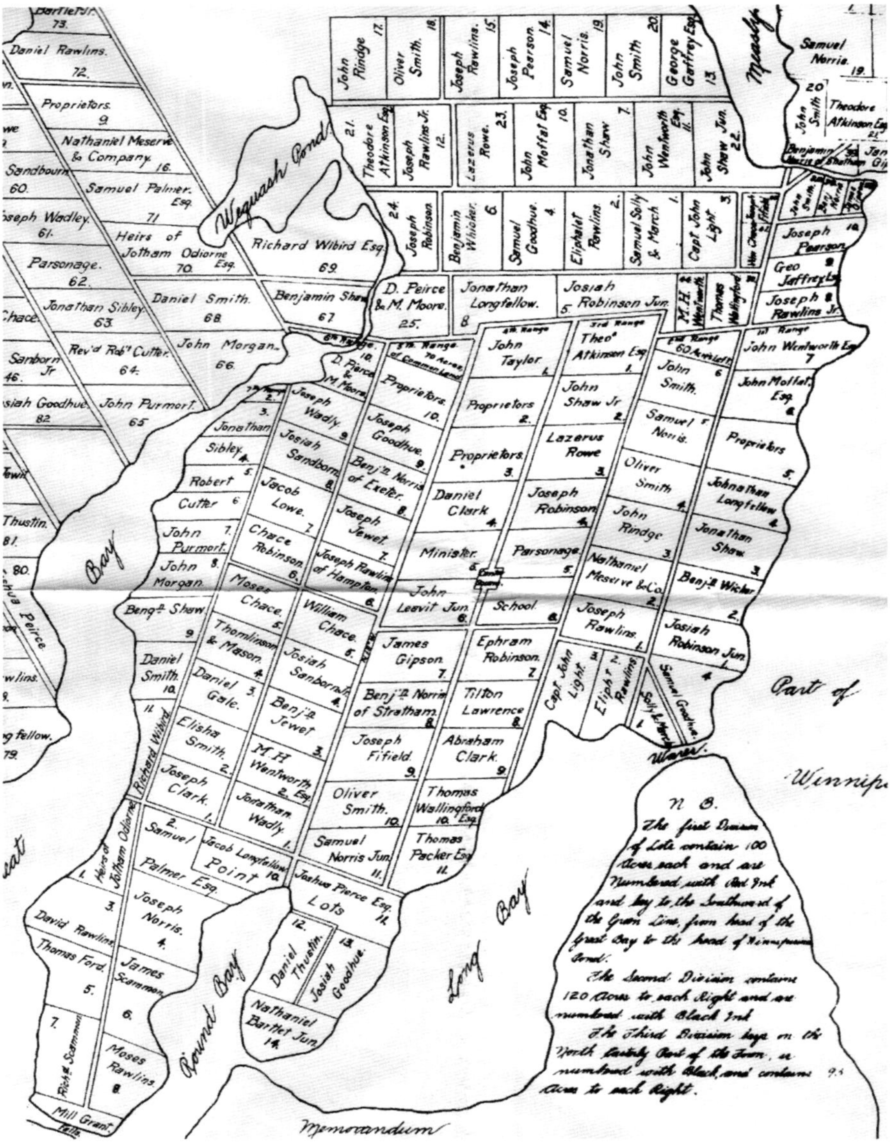

Surveyor's map of the town of Meredith, showing the first division of lots and ranges (center). *Meredith Historical Society.*

1754, they camped in the territory of today's Laconia and Meredith and ran straight survey lines over the rugged, forested ground, over obstacles and through bogs. Their equipment was a compass and staff for sighting and a sixty-six-foot-long Gunter's Chain for measuring distance. Trees were axe-blazed along the survey lines, and lot corners were axe-blazed on the in-facing surrounding "witness trees." The surveyors marked out some one hundred lots in the first of three divisions, neatly aligned in rows called "ranges." The proprietors of the new town then divided the lots among themselves, reserving designated lots for the support of a school and church and six acres for the town's administrative center. As originally granted, the town of Meredith contained a good deal of lake water, so in 1754, the proprietors of Meredith petitioned the Masonian Proprietors for more land. Their request was granted by the addition of Meredith Neck and land running all the way to current Center Harbor Village.

The proprietors who had received the grant of the town were men of substance who were living comfortably near the coast. They did not plan to settle in the wild new town themselves, but they wished to make a return on their investment by selling their lots to others. At first, many of those others were speculators, too, so lots changed hands, but no one settled on them. In 1760, the French lost both the war and Canada, raids ceased and the lands of the Lakes Region were finally safe to settle. However, there were no roads or any facilities, and actual settlers had still not appeared by 1764. The anxious proprietors then taxed themselves to raise the sum of £4,000 (British), which was to be divided equally among the first twenty of them to settle on their lots or find someone else to settle, clear land, build homes and stay for at least four years. They also voted to build a bridge across the Winnipesaukee River at current Laconia so that people could more easily enter the new town. To encourage settlement by families, the proprietors offered to grant 250 acres of land to the first child to be born there. By 1766, some twelve settlers had cleared land and built homes in the area, and by 1770, a sawmill and a gristmill were operating near the bridge.[8]

The man who benefited the most from the proprietors' inducements was Ebenezer Smith. He not only settled in town himself, bringing his wife, Sarah, and young son, Ebenezer Jr., but he brought three others to settle as well. He built his house at the corner of today's Parade Road and Elm Street in Laconia. Ebenezer's son Daniel was the second child to be born in town. Because the first child born was a girl, Ebenezer convinced the proprietors that Daniel should receive two hundred acres and the girl, Tamar Eaton, should receive only fifty.[9]

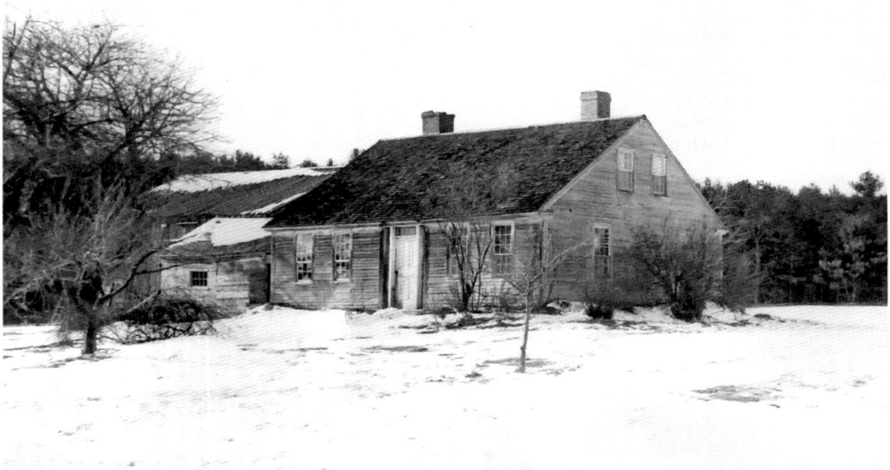

An old farm homestead. *Moultonborough Public Library Collection.*

Ebenezer Smith held many offices and wielded domineering power in the early town. He was proprietor's clerk, town clerk, justice of the peace, a selectman for many years, a colonel of militia and the representative to the legislature. He was one of the managers of the sawmill, and according to custom, the mill was entitled to one half of the lumber sawed for each settler who brought in logs. Lena Smith Ford wrote that in overseeing the annual tax assessments, Ebenezer "would take from the amount due some poor unfortunate man who had suffered losses and add it to that of a man able to pay. Strangely, no appeal was ever made from this action."[10] Ebenezer and Sarah had ten children, among whom he eventually divided his extensive landholdings. The Smith house no longer stands. It was described as a fine two-story house with a long ell connecting it to a twenty-four- by thirty-foot barn.

Other settlers were laboriously clearing land along today's Parade Road in what is now Laconia. The land the proprietors had set aside for a town center—with a meetinghouse, a school, a cemetery and a town pound for stray animals—was cleared at the current intersection of Parade and Pickerel Pond Roads. From the notes left by surveyors, who recorded which species of "witness trees" they axe-blazed at each lot corner, we know the kind of forest the settlers had to cut. They found mostly hardwoods—many beech trees, lesser numbers of maple and basswood and a bit of birch, oak, ash and elm. Intermixed were the more easily cut softwoods, hemlock and pine.[11] The

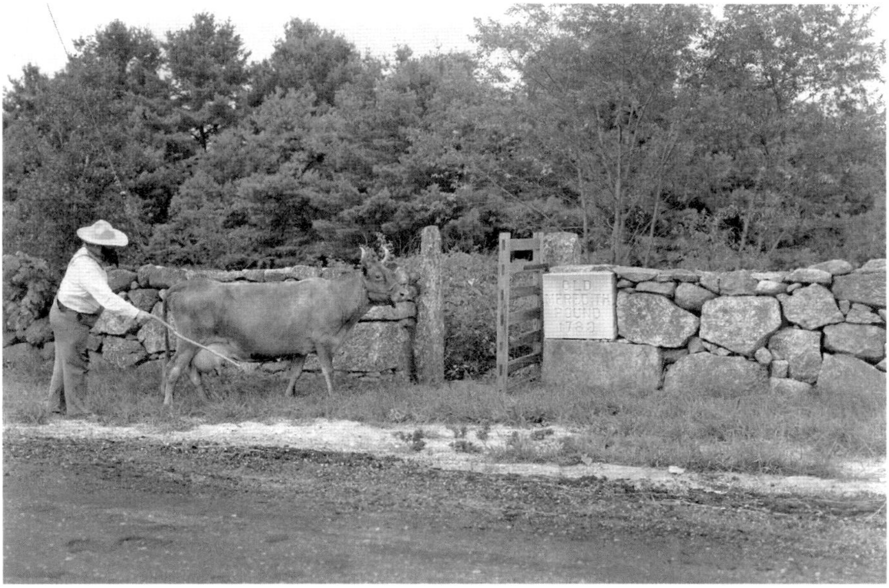

The Meredith town pound for stray animals at the old town square on Parade Road. *Meredith Historical Society.*

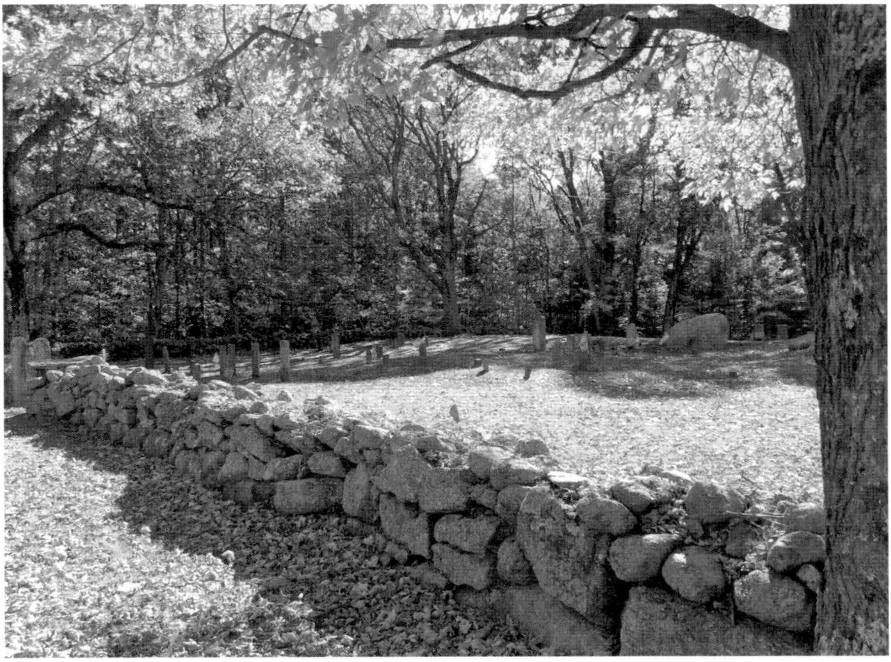

The original Meredith town square cemetery on Parade Road as it appears today. *Daniel Heyduk.*

trees, some with massive trunks, were felled with axes in the spring. Then the branches were cut off and laid on the ground to dry. White pine and any other logs intended for the sawmill or for cordwood were removed, and in late summer, everything left on the ground was set ablaze. Larger trunks and branches that did not burn completely were then cut into ten- to twelve-foot lengths, pulled into piles using skids and levers and burned again. The resulting wood ash was used to make soap, boiled down into potash for sale or left as fertilizer for crops to be planted among the stumps in the following year. Stumps had to be pulled and rocks removed before the land could be plowed, but much land was simply sown with grass for pasture.

The Province of New Hampshire conducted a census in 1767, but the settlers of future Meredith were too remote to be counted. Meredith (including Laconia) was given its present name and was officially incorporated as a town in the following year. By 1773, people had settled at more locations in the town, and the population had grown to 218 inhabitants. By 1786, the population had more than doubled to 572, and in the first U.S. Census in 1790, Meredith had 881 inhabitants.

Chapter 3

Early Roads, Taverns and the Mail

The first settlers arrived in Meredith by following a path through the forest marked by blazed trees. The cleared way was just wide enough for a horse or ox to pass, and indeed, it was said that Ebenezer Smith brought his wife, Sarah, and baby on a horse through the woods to their new home—with Ebenezer carrying a puppy in his pocket. A bridge was built in 1765 to cross the Winnipesaukee River at today's Laconia, then called Meredith Bridge, and that bridge served the Province Road. The road originated in a master plan by colonial governor John Wentworth to develop the interior of the province. Behind this plan was the reality that settlers in the north and west of the province would send their goods down the Connecticut River to Massachusetts unless roads linked them to the New Hampshire coast. Building the road was the fiscal and labor responsibility of the proprietors and residents of the towns through which it ran, and that made the result uneven to say the least.

According to provincial law, town surveyors were to lay out the route with compass and chain, finding the best path and water crossings, axe-marking trees along the way and leaving special marks as "mileposts." Then town-organized parties of axe men were to follow to clear the way wide enough for passage by a cart. By law, "all Male persons from Eighteen years of age" were liable for highway duty, with their teams of horses or oxen included. Tree stumps were to be cut close to the ground, and wet areas were to be made firm with logs laid crossways to the route. Pickaxes, shovels, hoes, crowbars and some gunpowder for blasting were used to create the road.

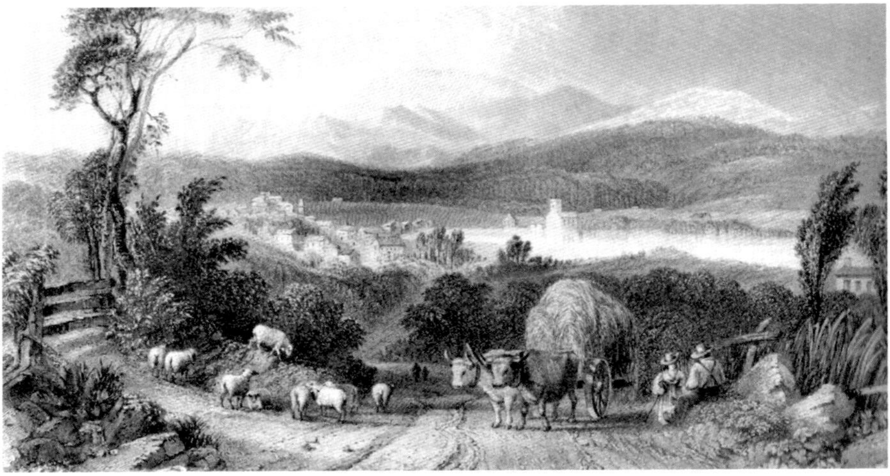

William Bartlett's sketch of Meredith Village and Meredith Bay from Ladd Hill, showing the Congregational church in its old location, 1830s. *The Old Print Barn.*

Such roads were rough and wet because of deep, organic forest soils and had widths too narrow to allow the sun to dry the roadbeds.[12]

In 1813, the village of Meredith Bridge had mills, businesses and Jonathan Folsom's Hotel, but there were still no wagons in use. The mail and all travel were on horseback, and sometimes three and even four people rode on a single horse.[13] The only through road was the Province Road, which seems to have been finished by 1770 and followed the route of Laconia's current Pleasant and North Main Streets and then current Parade Road, Pease Road and Winona Road through Meredith.

From the junction of today's Parade and Pease Roads, the Center Harbor Road (so called in deeds of the time) ran to Meredith Village. Laid out in 1773, this road offered a view north over Meredith Village and Meredith Bay as it descended Ladd Hill. In the 1830s, English artist William Henry Bartlett sketched this scene, and it later appeared in the book *American Scenery*. The Center Harbor Road continued through Meredith Village and north along Plymouth Street to avoid crossing the wide wetland where Hawkins Brook entered Lake Winnipesaukee (now filled in at Scenic Park). From Plymouth Street, the road turned east to cross Hawkins Brook near the cemetery and followed the higher ground to where True Road is today; then it continued on along the paths of today's Old Center Harbor and Sunset Hill Roads to reach Center Harbor Village. Those going to Meredith Neck turned south on True Road and continued south on today's Barnard Ridge Road, which ran as a "range road" between the surveyed lots on the Neck.[14]

Roads were traveled only in daylight. Not until 1792 were signposts required at intersections. There were fallen trees and washouts, and rivers and streams had to be forded. Ferries and bridges were few. The foot traveler might go fifteen miles in a day, and the horseback traveler might go thirty, but anyone using an ox cart to transport goods was limited to about ten miles per day. Stock being driven to market—including cattle, sheep, pigs, horses, mules, turkeys and geese—moved at the walking pace. At first, the occasional farmhouse was the only recourse for pasturing animals, obtaining food and passing the night, but by the 1780s and 1790s, taverns were appearing along these routes.[15]

Under such travel conditions, taverns were needed every ten to twelve miles and were officially licensed to maintain adequate stocks of beer and cider and to offer food and lodging, pasture, stable room, hay and feed. Failure to provide these could lead to loss of the license. The mail was carried along these roads, and taverns often became post offices, as well as sources of newspapers and official notices. On Parade Road, north of current Laconia, were the Davenport, Farrar and Young Taverns. Young's is the least well known, perhaps operating in colonial

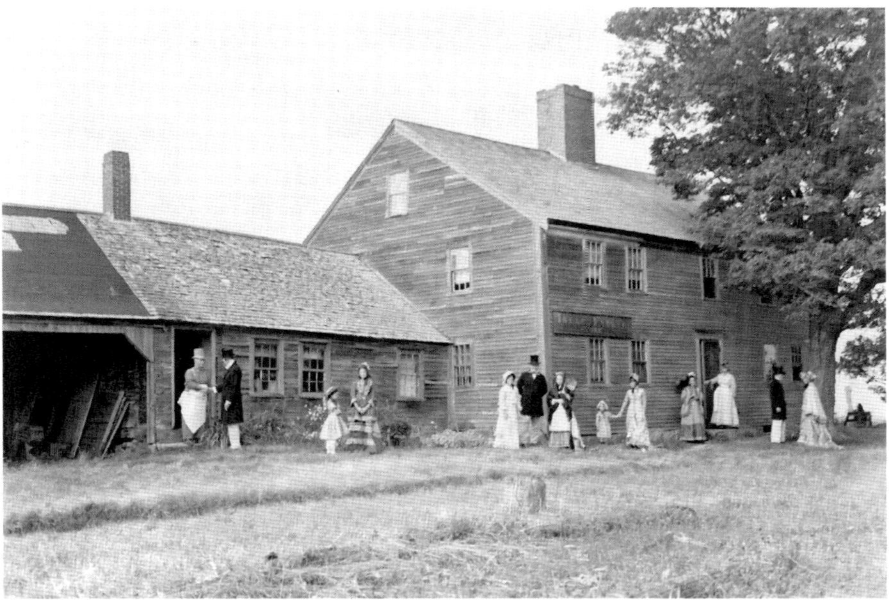

The Farrar Tavern on Parade Road. *Meredith Historical Society.*

times, while Farrar's was built sometime before 1782 and Davenport's was established after 1793.[16]

In colonial times, the mail was supervised by a postmaster general, and after the colonies declared independence in 1775, Benjamin Franklin was appointed to that office by the Continental Congress. The U.S. Postmaster General was concerned only with mail delivery among the states, and a New Hampshire Postmaster General was responsible for establishing post offices and laying out mail delivery routes within the state. He offered contracts to post riders to deliver newspapers and letters over designated routes in a specified period of time. One route began in Portsmouth, followed the Province Road north through Meredith and New Hampton to Plymouth and then turned west to Haverhill and continued down to Hanover before swinging east to return to Portsmouth through Boscawen. The rider needed to complete this circuit in two weeks. Because of the condition of the roads and water crossings, the job was only practical at first for a horse and rider, stopping at taverns en route to deliver and accept mail, eat, sleep and rest or change horses. Later, when the postal system was nationalized under the federal constitution, President Washington favored contracting stagecoach companies rather than individual riders because the coaches offered "a facility to the means of traveling [for the public]...a circumstance highly beneficial to any country." In effect, Washington saw mail contracts as helping public transportation.[17]

In 1825, the Winnepisiogee and White Mountain Mail Stage began service between Concord and Conway. The stage left Concord at 4:00 a.m. on Tuesdays and reached Conway by 6:00 p.m., passing through Gilford, Meredith, Center Harbor, Moultonborough and Sandwich along the way. These intermediate stops—including Meredith Bridge, the Davenport Tavern and Meredith Village—allowed for the horses to be changed and for the passengers to eat. The stage then returned on Wednesdays, leaving Conway at 4:00 a.m. for the fourteen-hour trip. The same service was repeated on Saturdays, with the return on Mondays. On the days that it was expected, the arrival of the stage was both a spectacle and a vital source of newspapers, the mail, new faces and word-of-mouth updates on affairs outside town.

From the late 1820s through the nineteenth century, most stagecoaches were the famous Concord coach, manufactured by Abbot-Downing Company of Concord. The curved wooden body of the coach was suspended from the wheeled carriage by multi-ply leather straps called "thorough-braces," which gave passengers a rocking rather than jolting

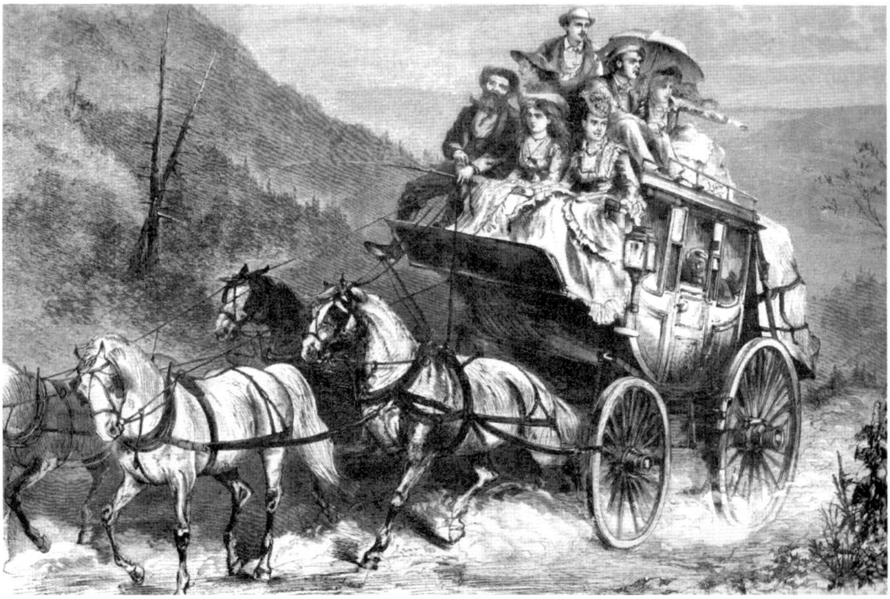

A Concord coach carrying tourists. *From* Harper's Weekly.

ride (Mark Twain called it a "cradle on wheels"). The coach was built strong to endure New Hampshire's rough roads and turnpikes, but the interior was a handsome combination of fine leather or plush, wood paneling and polished metal. Since glass windows were impractical, leather curtains were used instead. The exterior of the coach was elaborately painted, predominantly in red and yellow. Three sizes—for six, nine and twelve passengers—were available.[18]

After the railroad reached Meredith in 1849, stagecoaches still ran to Center Harbor, Moultonborough and Sandwich and on to North Conway. As a Meredith Village blacksmith in the late 1860s, Edgar Maloon remembered:

> *When the steamboats* Lady of the Lake *and the old* Davis *[Dover]* *began their regular trips* [in the summer], *the stage did not come to Meredith, but met the boats in Center Harbor.* [For] *a time in the fall and spring, the four and six horse stage would run to Meredith. The stage would come up to the hotel in great shape. Here they left all the team but the two pole horses. With these they delivered the mail at the post office and took passengers to the depot, then went back to the hotel, where a fresh team was*

hitched on and they started for North Conway. There were eighteen horses that were fed and shod here. Twelve were here and six were on the road all of the time. Every morning before eleven o'clock, my father and I shod six of them.[19]

Chapter 4

Dudley Leavitt and His *Farmer's Almanack*

Although his name is familiar and there is a historical marker for him on Route 25 at the Meredith-Center Harbor town line, Dudley Leavitt the man is less well known. He was born in Exeter, New Hampshire, in 1772 and attended school there, but he was mostly self-educated. Before coming to Meredith in 1806, Leavitt settled in Gilmanton, where he taught school, studied Greek and Latin with the minister, married Judith Glidden in 1795, started his *Farmer's Almanack* and a newspaper and served as selectman and town clerk. A deed dated 1801 shows that Dudley Leavitt, "Schoolmaster," bought one acre in Gilmanton from Andrew Glidden.

An October 2, 1806 deed shows that Dudley Leavitt, "husbandman," bought some forty-seven acres on Quarry Road, Meredith Neck, from Daniel Mead. This deed allowed Leavitt to choose his forty-seven acres from the "side or end of said lot," suggesting that the lot was undeveloped. Dudley, Judith and their four children moved to Meredith shortly thereafter. Their first home was a log cabin without a chimney, where an oven on a tree stump served their baking needs.[20] Dudley still produced the *Almanack* annually during this time. His daughter Jane was born in 1807, and in 1808, he signed the town tax inventory as one of the selectmen. Farmers who moved to new land in Meredith were hard-pressed to clear their land with axes and oxen in the first few years—without *also* researching and writing an almanac and serving as town selectman. In the following years, the Leavitts' log cabin was replaced by a "Cape Cod" wood-frame house, where four more children were born.[21]

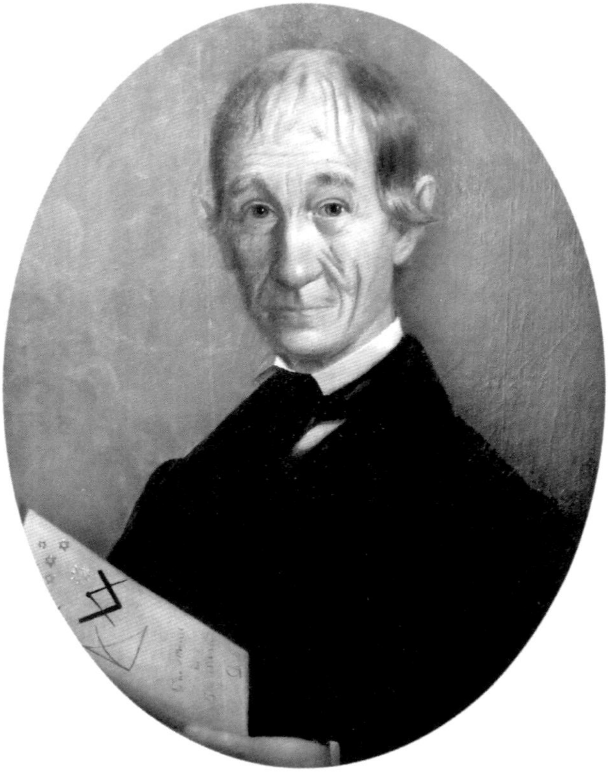

Left: A portrait of Dudley Leavitt—farmer, writer, scientist, teacher and mathematician—painted by Walter Ingalls. *Meredith Historical Society*.

Below: The Leavitt family's first frame house. *Meredith Historical Society*.

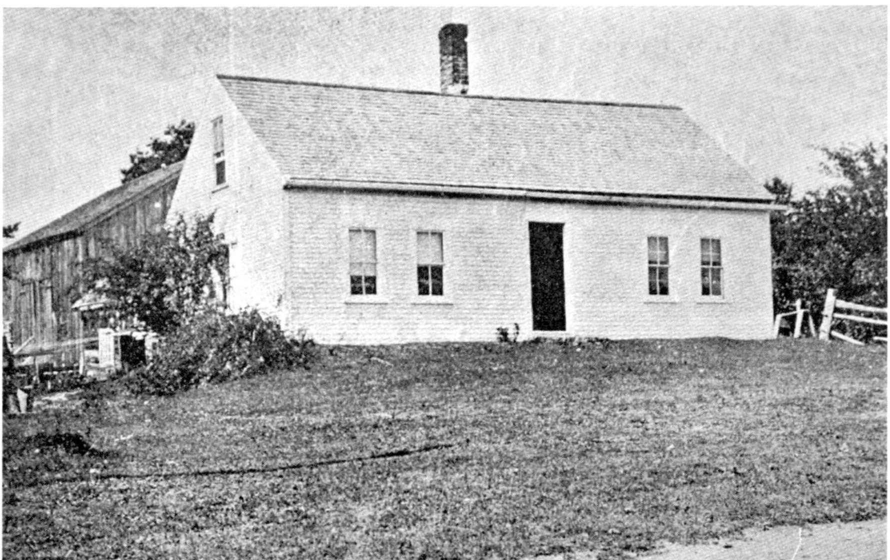

His farm established and his family growing, Dudley wrote a letter in the spring of 1811 offering to teach in the Meredith schools.[22] He taught in the public schools for some years and also ran his own private school, the Meredith Academick Academy, beginning in 1819. At that time, the Leavitts accepted boarding students in their new, larger home on Quarry Road, and Dudley charged tuition of "$3.00 per quarter, except for teaching algebra, navigation, gunnery, or the science of projectile, etc., spherick, geometry, and trigonometry, astronomy and philosophy for which the tuition will be $3.50 per quarter."[23] He wrote textbooks on English, arithmetic, astronomy and other subjects and submitted scientific papers to learned societies.

Deeds show that in 1813, 1817, 1821 and 1829, he bought more land, rounding out his farm to more than one hundred acres. Leavitt actively farmed his land, probably experimenting and putting the results in his almanac. He researched and wrote the *New England Farmer's Almanack* each year until his death in 1851. Even then, he left manuscripts for the next five years. The informative and entertaining almanac was a common fixture of New England kitchens, reaching a circulation of sixty thousand in the 1840s. One of the reasons for this popularity was that Dudley assumed a personal relationship with his readers and put much of his personality into what he wrote.

The *Farmer's Almanack* included predictions of the weather—"Windy" for January 29 and "Snow" for January 31, 1814—the time of sunrise and moonrise each day, the phases of the moon and notes about important historical events on that date. The almanac also had predictions of eclipses of the sun and moon, information about the planets and the stars, a chart of interest rates and postage rates and the dates on which the various courts of law would meet in each New England state. There was also a list of college vacation dates for the year. But to this staple information, Dudley added different personally written or selected pieces each year. One was a puzzle, the answer to which would appear in the following year's almanac. Another was his "Address to His Patrons," as this example from 1815 notes:

> [T]*he political fever has, for some time, been threatening us with an unfavorable termination, and now appears to have nearly approached to a crisis. Unless a speedy union take place between the political parties* [of the United States] *who have long been so unhappily opposed to each other, how can we expect, how can we even hope for prosperous and happy times?*

In the almanac of 1814, he wrote an essay on "Envy": "[I]t is an eternal truth, that envy desires not so much its own happiness as another's misery";

there was also one on "The Benefits of Adversity": "[I]f our strength is double, we are as much relieved as if half our burden was taken away." There was poetry, too, such as "On Study": "Poetic fields encompass me around/And still I seem to tread on classic ground/I vow'd to the muses, my time and my care/Since neither could win me the smiles of the fair."

Dudley wrote of the actual weather of the year past: "In 1845, in New Hampshire the spring was backward, and at Meredith the ice did not disappear in Winnipisiogee lake until the sixth day of May. On the twenty-second of April the frogs peeped, as much as to say, Here we are again." He wrote about how to grow various crops, treatments for diseases in people and animals, how to dye cloth and "how to clean gloves without wetting them." In the almanac of 1838, he provided a list of all the stagecoaches that ran from Concord, with their stops and days of operation. When the railroad was completed to Meredith in 1849, Dudley listed the fare to each station all the way to Boston (e.g., Weirs, ten cents; Lowell, two dollars). In 1850, the year before his death, he gave "Advice to Young Ladies": "Learn to work, and not be dependent upon servants."

The year of 1816 had frost in every month and came to be known in New England as the "year without a summer." People in Meredith and throughout New England had Dudley Leavitt's time-proven *Almanack* to tell them what weather to expect. He prepared that almanac in the spring of 1815, using predictive sources that he had used since 1797. He could not have known of the April 1815 eruption of Mount Tambora in Indonesia, the most explosive eruption in recorded history and the source of a high-altitude cloud of sulfur and fine ash that would affect global weather the following year. In any case, the effects of volcanism on climate were then unrecognized.

The weeks between January and March 1816 were not unusual. For April, the *Almanack* predicted average temperatures and above-average rain, but cold and dry conditions actually occurred. Dudley predicted "perhaps a cold May" overall, marking May 14 and 15 as "fair and warm." The month was indeed "cold and very backward," but rather than "warm" on May 15, many New Hampshire locations saw unexpected frost and snow. He predicted early June to be "fair and temperate" and "very warm" on June 23 and 24. June did indeed begin with warm weather, but from June 6 to 11 there were "very cold winds and large frost," and snow fell in many locations. Then, on June 23, temperatures reached near ninety degrees, just as the *Almanack* had suggested. It was to be "hot and sultry" from July 5 to 7, according to Leavitt, and then "cool for the season" from July 15 to 17.

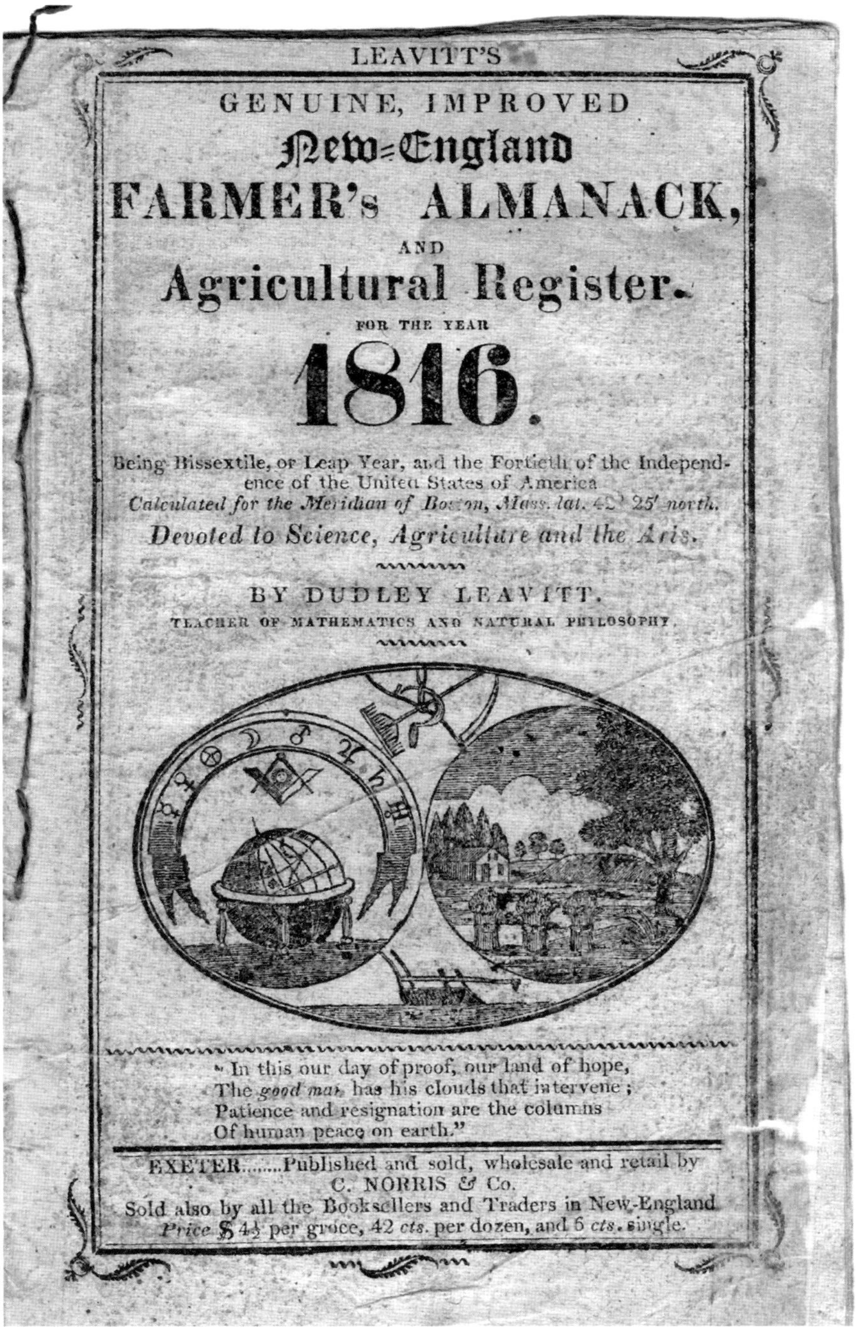

LEAVITT'S

GENUINE, IMPROVED

New-England

FARMER's ALMANACK,

AND

Agricultural Register.

FOR THE YEAR

1816.

Being Bissextile, or Leap Year, and the Fortieth of the Independence of the United States of America

Calculated for the Meridian of Boston, Mass. lat. 42° 25′ north.

Devoted to Science, Agriculture and the Arts.

BY DUDLEY LEAVITT.

TEACHER OF MATHEMATICS AND NATURAL PHILOSOPHY.

"In this our day of proof, our land of hope,
The *good man* has his clouds that intervene;
Patience and resignation are the columns
Of human peace on earth."

EXETER........Published and sold, wholesale and retail by
C. NORRIS & Co.
Sold also by all the Booksellers and Traders in New-England.
Price \$4½ per groce, 42 *cts.* per dozen, and 6 *cts.* single.

Leavitt's *Farmer's Almanack* for 1816, the "year without a summer." *Meredith Historical Society.*

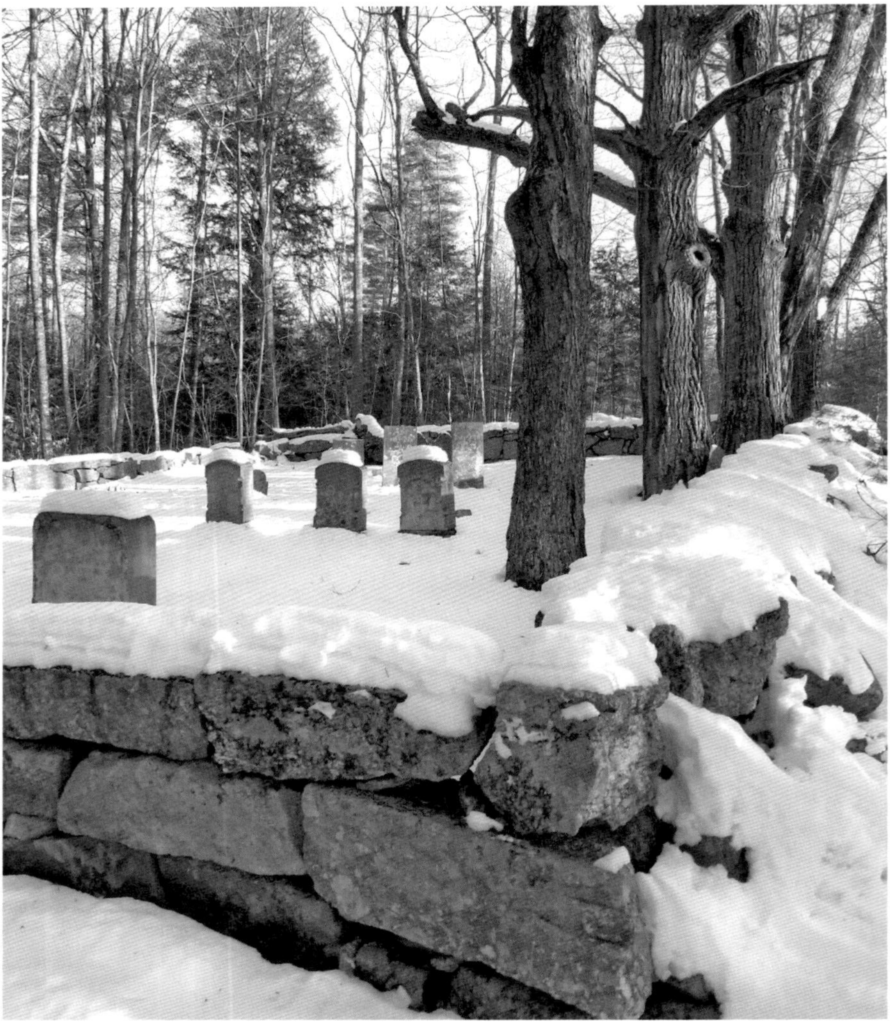

The Leavitt family cemetery near Page Pond and Forest, as it appears today. *Daniel Heyduk.*

There was indeed a warm early July, but then came "white frost" on July 8. July 17 did prove to be cool and rainy, as the *Almanack* had suggested. For August, Dudley Leavitt predicted a warm month, with "variable weather" from August 27 to 30. The first three weeks of the month were just as he expected, but then widespread frost struck on August 21 and it remained cold through the end of the month—somewhat like his prediction, but much worse in degree. The *Almanack* foresaw fair weather for early

September and then "foul weather and chilly air" from September 5 to 8 and "frosty mornings" and "cool evenings" from September 18 to 21. The early month was indeed fair, but September 11 saw snow, and hard frosts occurred from September 20 through the end of the month, where "hazy sky and smoky air" had been predicted.[24]

The weather of 1816 was made more ominous by the appearance of dark spots on the surface of the sun that could be seen with the naked eye. In the next year's almanac, Dudley suggested that those spots were related to the weather. In fact, the sun was at a low point in its regular cycle of sunspot activity (a "Dalton Minimum"), but the volcanic cloud of 1816 had apparently made sunspots more visible. Leavitt could not be blamed for failing to predict the "year without a summer." In fact, he was accurate for about half the summer, missing the extraordinary plunges in temperature that came suddenly and sporadically. He did not predict the unusually dry conditions that led to forest fires in September and October. But in an essay in the 1816 *Almanack*, he wrote, "In New England, the state of New Hampshire in particular, frosts have been known in every month of the year excepting July." He also wrote that on May 19, 1815, "[I]t began to snow, and continued to do so with every appearance of a December storm, so that the snow lay upon the ground from three to four inches deep." Some local farmers, perhaps heeding those words, decided to plant wheat or rye instead of corn in 1816. Those who did harvested a crop, while those who planted corn lost it to the frosts and snow.

Dudley and Judith lived on their Meredith farm from 1806 until the end of their lives. As was customary at that time, the Leavitts created a family cemetery on their farm. The first to be buried there was an eight-year-old daughter, followed by an eighteen-year-old son and then thirty-one-year-old Dudley Jr. In time, both Dudley and Judith were buried there, as were their descendants who continued to farm the surrounding land. The last to do so was great-grandson Dudley Leavitt, who deeded Leavitt Park to the Town of Meredith at his death in 1945.

Chapter 5

The Cider and Other Taxes

On May 23, 1808, Meredith selectmen Daniel Smith, Moses Plumer and Dudley Leavitt sent the town tax inventory to the state. In doing so, they knew that the farm acreage they reported was not the actual acreage that the farmers owned. They were not breaking the law; in the taxes of the day, an acre of pasture was not a measured acre but rather one-fourth of a cow. This had been so since 1777, it continued to be so until 1833 and it had to do with farming.

At that time, virtually all Meredith settlers were farmers. Some farms were on rich bottomland, while others were thin-soiled and rocky, making acreage of farmland much less important than quality of farmland. Every farm needed to have a tilled field for crops, pasture for the essential cows, horses and oxen to graze in the summer, mowing fields for hay to feed those animals in the winter and an orchard to produce enough cider for the family to drink year-round. Each of those things was taxed, but not by its market value.

To be fair to all farmers, the state tax system measured acreage by production: one acre of tilled land was defined as the amount of land needed to produce "25 bushels of Indian corn," one acre of mowing was the amount of land needed to produce "1 ton of English hay," one acre of orchard was the space needed to produce "10 barrels of cider," and pasture land was determined by counting the farmer's cows—each cow equaled four acres of pasture. On a rich-soiled farm, an acre that produced fifty bushels of corn was taxed as two acres, and on a poor-soiled farm, the two acres that were needed to produce twenty-five bushels were taxed as one acre. The assessor asked how many barrels of cider the farm produced and converted that to acres of orchard. Farmers also were taxed on their horses, oxen and cows, with older animals taxed more than younger ones, according to the number of winters they had passed.

In addition, the "poll [head] tax" was levied on all men between the ages of eighteen and seventy, except "those 18 to 21 years old in the militia; ordained ministers; the president, professors, tutors and students of colleges; paupers and idiots." Women and children were not taxed as "polls" because they did not vote. Houses and barns were not taxed, nor was "unimproved wildland," but mills were, as they were productive.

Each town was given an apportionment of the state tax levy, and the selectmen were responsible for reporting the total "polls," the total tilled, pasture, mowing and orchard land, as well as all the taxable animals in the town. Meredith's 1807 town tax inventory listed 302 polls (out of about 1,800 residents), 95 acres of orchard, 300 acres of tillage, 1,124 acres of mowing and 2,694 acres of pasture. Of animals three years or older, 355 horses, 424 oxen and 930 cows and cattle were reported. The town collected the tax and sent its apportioned share to the state. By law, selectmen who knowingly underreported the town inventory were to pay the difference from their own pockets.

Tax records were only roughly accurate for acres of cleared land, but they do tell us that Meredith farms were mostly stock farms, with little land devoted to crops. If we include the hundreds of unrecorded animals under three years old, there were more animals in Meredith than people in 1807. Anyone who was interested could find out a good deal about a resident's farm from the public tax record of the time.

At that time, almost everyone drank cider daily, so there were great quantities of it in town, and the tax on it was significant. Apples had been brought from Europe by the first New England settlers, along with honeybees, which the Native Americans called "English flies." There were reported to be apple trees growing at the Weirs that the Native Americans had obtained from the settlers before 1700. When the settlers arrived, they carried seeds and bare-root stock to plant at their new homes, and there were many varieties of apples from the start—early and late maturing and sweet and tart. In early Meredith, virtually every farm had an orchard of apples and pears, and the main product of these was fermented cider from the apples and "perry" from the pears.

Esther Carleton Wyatt, who grew up on a farm in Meredith in the 1920s, remembered that "there were quite a number of very good apple trees on

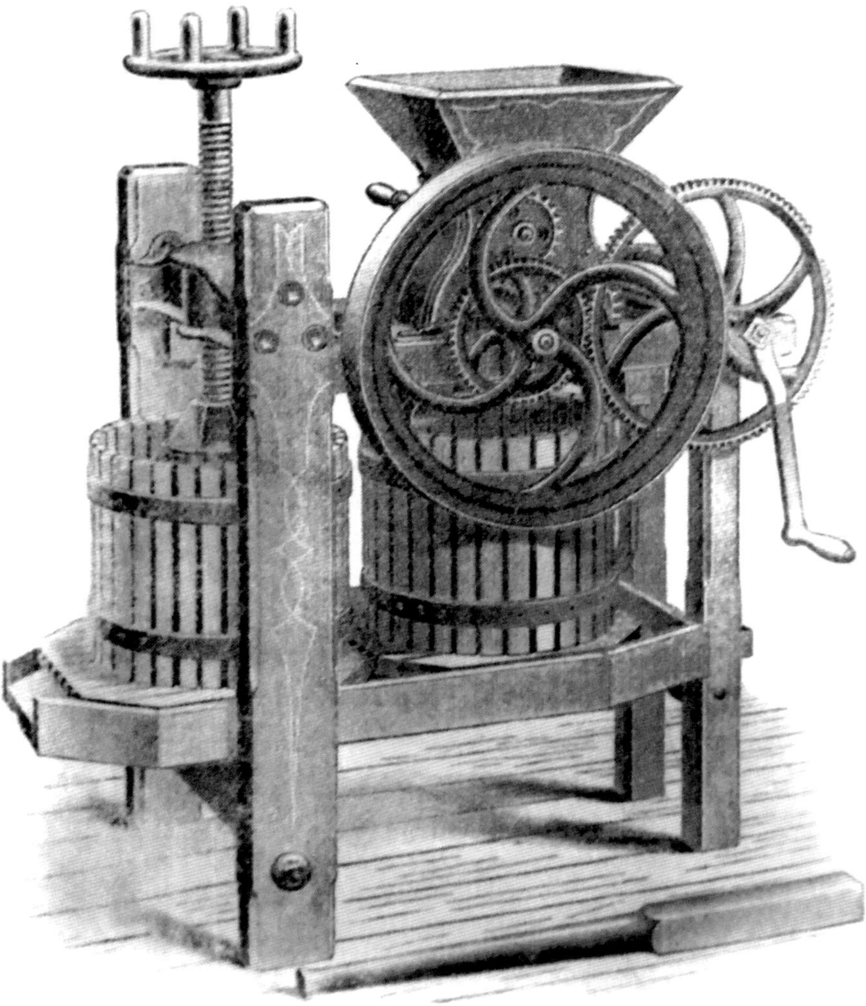

A hand-operated cider mill used to crush the apples (right) and then press cider from the pomace (left). *Meredith Historical Society Farm Museum.*

the farm, set by some previous owner many years before. Despite the little care they received from my father, no pruning, spraying or extra fertilizer, they usually produced well if the weather cooperated too." She remembered filling barrels with Baldwins, Greenings, Winter Bananas and other varieties for storage in the cellar. Such mixed orchards were useful for blending apples for cider, for having particular apples for special purposes and for the overall survival of the orchard from apple diseases and blights. After the unblemished storage apples were carefully picked and put away, the cider apples were shaken from the tree and collected from the ground; "wild" pasture apples were collected as well. Esther explained that "these too had to be picked up before the cows could get to them. "A cow would eat on the apples until it became drunk," which "usually caused the cow to dry up and no longer produce milk."[25]

Apples contain natural yeasts that cause fermentation and preserve the (hard) cider for long-term use. First the apples were crushed into a mash called "pomace" in a hand-cranked mill. Some juice was collected, but most came from wrapping the pomace in cloth and pressing it in a home screw press. The juice was then barreled, with the bung left open, and it fermented over several weeks. Cider improved with age, and if the farmer waited until the following spring or early summer, a second fermentation took place that reduced the sharpness of the drink. All taverns served cider, and farm families drank it with every meal. For children, water was added to make "ciderkin."

In 1833, the state legislature changed the tax system from one based on production to one based on the value of property. From that time on, land, houses and farms were assessed an overall value—and orchards were included. In addition, "polls" and livestock were still recorded and taxed. As many Meredith farms scaled down production and lost income during the later nineteenth century, the tax based on property value became more burdensome.

Chapter 6

When Women Were Invisible

For the time up to 1850, the Meredith records available to us mostly involve men. During that time, men were the principal property owners, and deeds recorded transactions between them: Mr. A, of Exeter, husbandman, bought fifty acres from Mr. B, of Meredith, gentleman. If these men were married, their wives did not enter into it, except to "relinquish their right of dower." Married women did not own property jointly with their husbands, but by long usage, a widow was entitled to one-third of her deceased husband's property for her support. This was her right of dower, also known as "the widow's third." To give a buyer clear title to property, the seller's wife would sometimes officially relinquish her one-third claim, which entered her name on the deed. The buyer's wife remained invisible.

In the taxes of that time, all men over the age of eighteen were subject to the "poll tax" and, by virtue of paying it, were entitled to vote. Thus, voter rolls recorded only men. Property was taxed, too, and for that purpose, assessors recorded productive land, livestock, "chaises," mills, ferries and bridges by the name of the owner—again, usually a man. Except for the occasional widow, women did not appear in the tax records.

From the first United States census in 1790 through the census of 1840, households were recorded under the name of the "head of household"—almost always a man, except for a few widows. The census was greatly interested in the gender and ages of other members of the household but did not record their names. The household head's wife, nameless in the census, could usually be identified by her gender and age, except if the head remarried, and then a new, younger wife might be mixed in with the daughters. In the 1850 census, for the first time, the names of all members of a household were taken down, and from then on, the numbers became real people—named grandparents, parents, children, in-marrying spouses, grandchildren, boarders, nurses and servants.

Identifying women in Meredith history before 1850 requires sources other than deeds, tax rolls or the census. Much genealogical work has been done using birth, marriage and death records, and it is here that the women and children are to be found. Family ties were very important during that time, often influencing where people lived, who they married, what occupation they followed and how they inherited property. Having the names of wives and mothers shows us the whole families in which people lived—the families in which they solved problems and made decisions.

Women were seen less in public than men were, partly because of being outside the property, tax and political systems and partly because of their home-based activities. At that time, it was common for a woman to bear eight to twelve children. Women worked at home doing things that would later become industrialized: processing flax into linen cloth; carding, spinning and weaving wool; preserving food, cooking from "scratch"; making candles; and producing soap, butter and cheese for home and market. They joined the outdoor work at planting and harvest and especially at haying and cider-making. Women also were responsible for making medicines and "doctoring" family members.

Since women produced most of the cloth, it is not surprising that when the first textile mills appeared in the early nineteenth century, women were predominantly the millworkers. By the 1830s, many women who would have woven cloth at home were mass-producing it in the textile mills of Meredith Bridge, Meredith Center and Meredith Village. Traditionalists like state senator Isaac Hill lamented in 1832 that "the farmer's daughters are obliged to herd together in fifties, hundreds and thousands in the manufacturing establishments, or if they remain at home, no longer find that profitable and wholesome employment which was so highly beneficial to the prosperity and to the morals of the whole community."[26] Along with providing economic independence, the mills later also offered social, artistic and educational opportunities that began to bring women more into the public sphere.

A public role in which women figured prominently in Meredith was that of teaching in the many one-room schools. As the town grew in population, so did the number of school districts, reaching twenty-three schools in 1845, when Meredith still included Laconia and part of Center Harbor. Even in

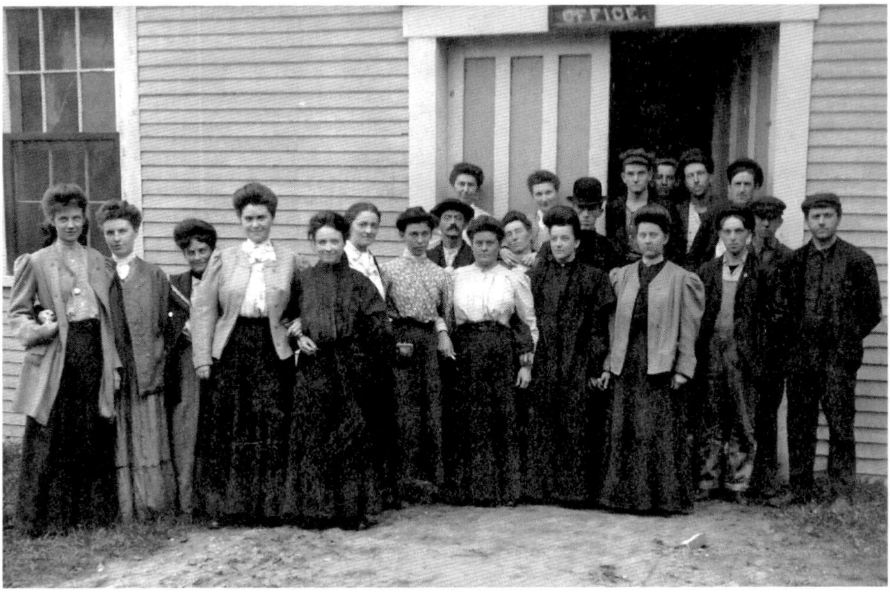

Spinning room workers at the Meredith Linen Mill, circa 1900. *Meredith Historical Society.*

1900, without Laconia and with land in the east given to Center Harbor, Meredith had seventeen school districts. Teachers were usually young single women who boarded with families in the district during the school term. Of fourteen teachers in Meredith in the 1860 census, eleven were women. While they held sway in the classroom, teachers had little free time and virtually no privacy during the school week. They taught all subjects to all ages of children, and most children received no further education beyond the district school. In 1848, one woman taught reading, writing, arithmetic, natural philosophy, history, algebra and surveying.[27] Female teachers were paid less than men and were assumed to be cheaper to board. In the Meredith–Center Harbor Union School District in 1844, the weekly board was set at $1.29 for the schoolmaster and $0.99 for the schoolmistress.[28]

Edgar Maloon of Meredith Village remembered going as a boy in the 1850s to be cared for by Mary Ellen Smith, who "had a room where she took care of and amused the little tots while their mothers did their work." Edgar also remembered working in Meredith Village's cotton stocking mill as a boy of eleven years old in the 1860s, and he named the thirteen mill girls who worked with him in the room where the raw cotton was fed into "willowing" machines, which fluffed it up. Other girls worked in the pressing

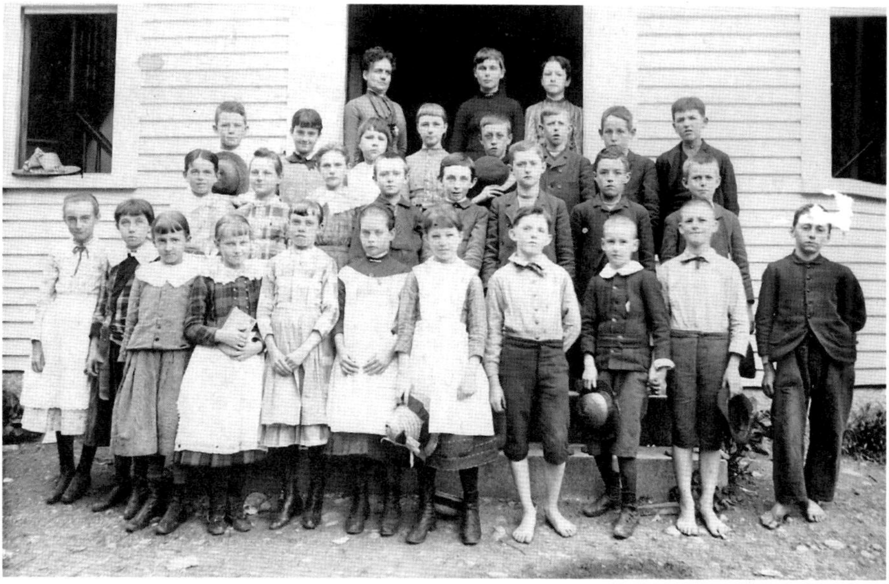

Schoolchildren and their teacher, Ella Beede (left, rear), 1800s. *Meredith Historical Society.*

room, the hand-sewing room, the boxing room and perhaps in other rooms where he did not.[29]

That mill closed, but by 1880, women were living in boardinghouses in Meredith Village and working in the Hodgson Hosiery Mill, which employed "from one hundred fifty to one hundred sixty operatives, the greater number of whom are women and natives of the vicinity."[30] Women began to take on more public roles in the latter part of the nineteenth century. Many were active in the temperance and suffrage movements, where they organized, lectured and marched. The national Grange movement, which came to Meredith with the founding of the Winnipesaukee Grange in 1875 and the Lake Wicwas Grange in 1901, enrolled women and reserved certain offices exclusively for them.

Married women did not have separate property rights until the 1850s, when the legislature passed laws making married women's wills valid, allowing banks to make payments directly to women rather than their husbands and allowing the wives of insane men to hold property in their own right. The right to vote was hardest to achieve. A 1902 women's suffrage referendum in New Hampshire was voted down. In an article in the *Ladies Home Journal* of October 1905, former U.S. president and Tamworth summer resident Grover Cleveland wrote, "The relative positions to be assumed by men and women in the working out of our civilization were assigned long ago by a higher intelligence." He continued: "Sensible and responsible women do not want to vote." New York State gave women full suffrage in 1917. The first national election in which Meredith women could vote was that of 1920.

Chapter 7

PAGE POND AND FOREST

The Settlers, the Quarry and the Mill

Meredith's public Page Pond and Forest on Meredith Neck is a museum of Meredith history. There is no sign that Native Americans lived there, but they did live nearby on Stonedam Island. They undoubtedly hunted and trapped along Page Brook and its series of wetlands, and they probably cut birch bark, black spruce roots and the wood of cedar, ash and maple to make their canoes. Beaver are active along Page Brook again today, as they were before the ruinous colonial demand for their pelts, and moose, bears, bobcats, mink, otter, turkeys and many other casualties of the clearing of the land have also returned.

In 1754, the Meredith proprietors asked the Masonian proprietors for more land, and the latter obliged by extending the town's north boundary to the east for five more miles. This brought Meredith Neck into the town, and it was surveyed into lots of some ninety-five acres each by 1770. The survey map shows the lots laid out in rows, or "ranges," running from southwest to northeast in a pattern that roughly crosses the width of the Neck—the best way to get the greatest number of equal-sized lots. Roads called "rangeways" were to separate these rows of lots, but most of these roads were never built.

Part of today's Blueberry Hill Road is an original rangeway that divided the survey lots of the sixth and seventh ranges. The old rangeway, now a dirt woods road, enters Page Pond and Forest and reaches the forested site of the Gilman homestead, marked by the cellar hole of the house, the sills of the barn and sheds and a stone-lined water well. Revolutionary War veteran James Gilman bought all ninety-five acres of lot 51 on the northwest side of the rangeway in 1789. He also bought lot 57 on current Meredith Neck Road. James, his wife, Deborah, and their children moved from Newmarket to settle on one of these lots in 1790. The Gilman family grew, and James

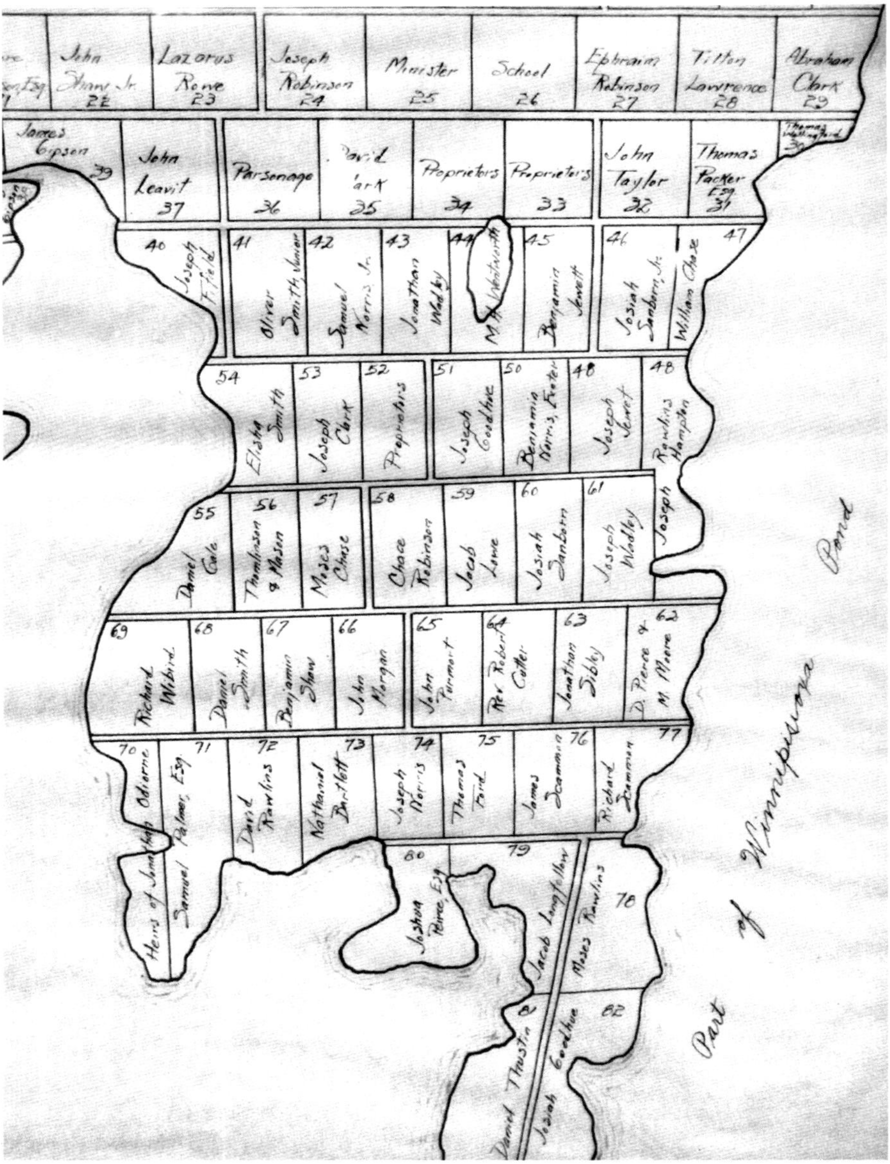

Survey map of Meredith Neck, showing numbered lots and the first owners, few of whom ever settled there. *Meredith Historical Society.*

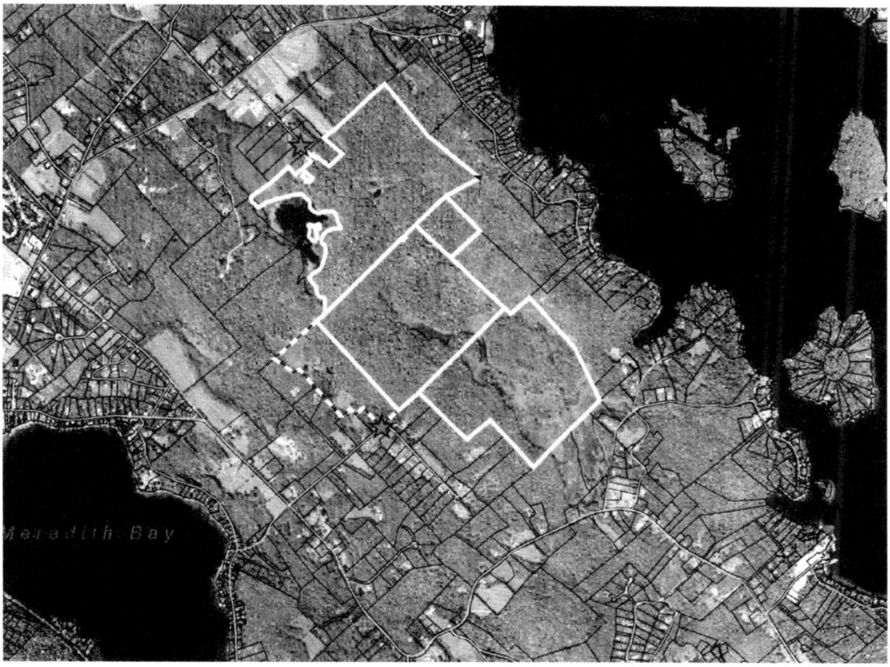

An aerial view of Meredith Neck showing Page Pond and Forest, which today includes several original survey lots. *Meredith Conservation Commission.*

later bought lot 50. His grandson, James, married Susan Mead in 1836 and in that same year bought one-half of lot 60. The land, now in Page Pond and Forest, later passed to David Gilman. It is not clear who first lived at the homestead marked by the cellar hole, but David; his wife, Lucy; and their children—Clara, John, David and Mary—were living in that house and farming there in 1859.[31] The house was in one lot, and the barn was across the rangeway in another. When David passed the barn lot to Granville and Mary Gilman in 1890, he reserved the right to use the barn and "the yard that belongs to the barn as now fensed."

To the north of the Gilman land, the original survey shows Page Pond in lot 44 and the land of lot 45 lying to the east. These lots are at the north limit of current Page Pond and Forest. Today's Quarry Road, which passes Moulton farm, was built as a road between rangeways, separating original lots 33 and 34. At the foot of Quarry Road was a rangeway—now abandoned—that ran along the northwest boundary of lot 45, and it was at that spot that Dudley and Judith Leavitt settled in 1806. They later built a larger house just to the north, and their original house was sold and moved in about 1825; the family cemetery is there, with the graves of Dudley, Judith and three more generations. The Leavitts' descendants—son Isaac and his wife, Sarah; grandson Arthur and his wife, Elizabeth; and great-grandson Dudley—lived there and farmed the family land for some 140 years. Last to do so was bachelor Dudley, who occupied the homestead with his aunt, Hulda, and his sisters, Mary Alice and Marion.

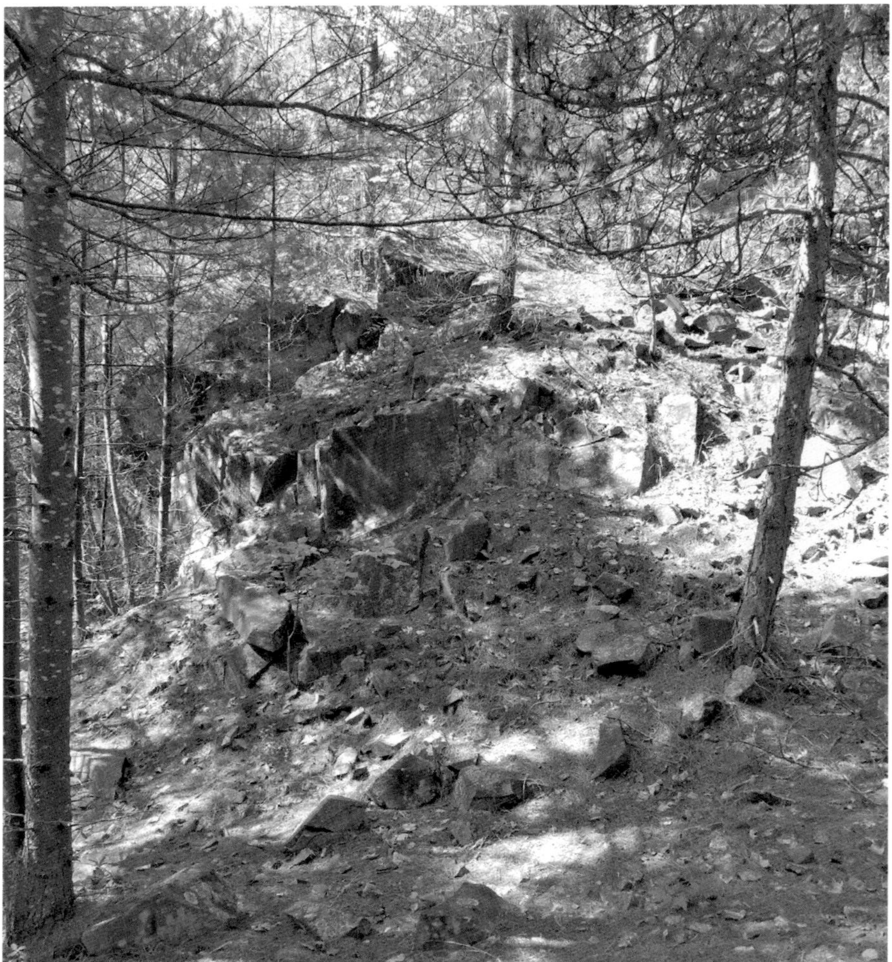

Forest has reclaimed the abandoned traprock quarry on former Leavitt family land, now in Page Pond and Forest. *Daniel Heyduk.*

Dudley was active in the Winnipesaukee Grange, a dedicated farmer and a breeder of oxen, which he showed in Meredith and at the annual Plymouth Fair. He was town supervisor and a representative to the legislature. During his ownership of the farm in the 1920s, "traprock" was found to underlie the land to the south of the family cemetery. This dark, igneous rock was ideal to crush for use in building road and railroad beds. A quarry was created on the Leavitt land where the rock was blasted and crushed on site and then transported out via Quarry Road. Now abandoned, and a striking feature of Page Pond and Forest, the quarry was operated for a time by the state. Dudley died in 1945 and deeded Leavitt Park beach to the town in his will. The town acquired Page Pond and Forest separately in 2010. Visitors today can see the quarry pits and some of the old quarry equipment.

An impressive cut-stone milldam—ninety-six feet long, sixteen feet wide and eighteen feet high—now sits deep in the woods along Page Brook. It dates from 1830 or shortly thereafter, when James Gilman sold a small piece of land along Fish Brook, "a few rods southwesterly of the outlet of the little pond," to Sewall Leavitt. Title to this land included a "mill privilege," which

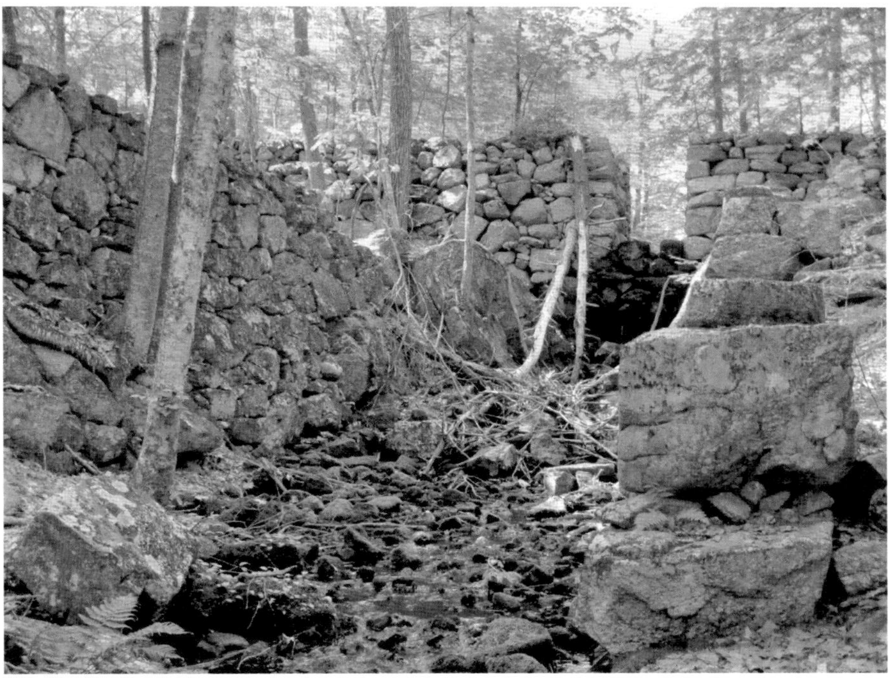

The stone milldam across Page Brook, where a sawmill once operated. *Daniel Heyduk.*

allowed Leavitt to build a dam and flood the land of his upstream neighbor, Dr. Jeremiah Morgan, until May 20 of each year. He built the dam and a water-powered sawmill, which he operated until selling the mill and the two-and-a-half-acre mill parcel to John Page in 1836. Page operated the mill until 1855. Fish Brook came to be known as Page Brook, and Little Pond, which provided water power to the mill, came to be called Page Pond. John Page did not live at the mill site but rather at the bottom of today's Blueberry Hill Road, which was then known as Page Road.

Edwin Moulton, late owner of Moulton farm, was told by his grandfather that the carriage that held the saw log in the mill was operated by two chains from the waterwheel axle—one to pull the carriage ahead toward the single up-and-down saw blade and the other to pull it back after the log was cut. He was also told that the beams, square and long, which were used to build nearby barns, came from this mill.[32] The sawmill was probably quite active while farm construction was taking place, especially during the sheep boom of the 1830s and 1840s, but building work died down after that. Up-and-down blade sawmills gave way to much faster rotary blade mills in Meredith in the 1860s, and the remote Page Brook mill was probably not modernized. Portable steam-powered mills also came into use at that time. The Page mill passed to James Bickford, who owned an adjoining farm, and he, in turn, sold the property, with no mention of a mill building, to David Gilman in 1879. David was the great-grandson of James Gilman, who had originally sold the mill parcel to Sewall Leavitt. David's daughter Clara sold the land in 1904 to the Meredith Shook and Lumber Company for its timber value. From that time until the purchase of Page Pond and Forest by the town, the land surrounding the old mill site was managed as woodlot, and the dam was a rumored curiosity seen by few. The 180-year-old dam, built of dry-laid stone, still holds back the water of the millpond behind it today.

Chapter 8

Water Power, Mills and Villages in Growing Meredith

At the time the town of Meredith was laid out, the centrally located flatland along present Parade Road in Laconia was chosen by the proprietors as the administrative center. The Meredith town square, the meetinghouse and a school were to be located there. However, that site lacked a permanent fall of water to power the essential sawmills and gristmills that were needed for building houses and barns and to grind the settlers' grain. In 1765, a sawmill was built on the Winnipesaukee River at current Laconia, which was then called Meredith Bridge. The proprietors authorized Ebenezer Smith and William Mead to run the mill for three years. Their compensation was that they kept half of the boards and framing lumber sawed there. Their sawmill took advantage of the fact that the Winnipesaukee River dropped twenty feet between Paugus Bay and Lake Winnisquam. Abraham Folsom also tapped this power to build a sawmill and a gristmill at current Lakeport in about 1780.[33]

The water power closest to the planned town square was located to the north, where Lake Wicwas's water dropped some twenty feet into Lake Winnisquam at current Meredith Center. In 1767, the proprietors offered forty pounds and a "mill privilege" to whoever would build a mill there along today's Mill Brook. By 1770, Joshua Folsom had built a gristmill, and later, Captain Noah Lawrence built a sawmill. The road from the town square to Meredith Center was originally known as the "Mill Path," and Meredith Center was called Lawrence's Mills, Bickford's Mills and Chase's Mills after successive mill owners. A fourth source of water power in the new

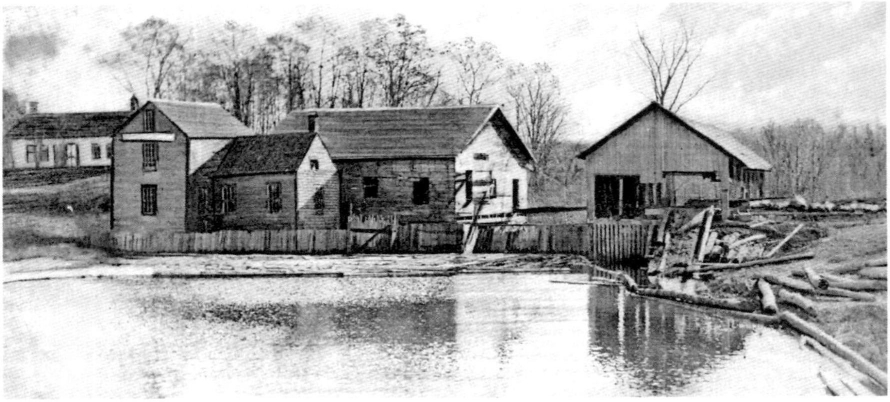

The water-powered mills at the dam across Mill Brook in Meredith Center village. *Meredith Historical Society*.

town was the forty-foot drop from Measley Pond (Lake Waukewan) to Lake Winnipesaukee at current Meredith Village. Gristmills and sawmills were built there along Measley Pond Brook, which ran from Lake Waukewan through today's lumberyard and past the fire department to empty into Lake Winnipesaukee near the town docks.[34]

The Meredith meetinghouse was built as planned on Parade Road, but economic development was taking place at the water power sites, each of which became a village. Soon after 1800, Daniel Avery built the first cotton mill at Meredith Bridge, and a carding mill was also built there. Additional water-powered businesses at Meredith Bridge were Daniel Tucker's tool-making forge and trip hammer in 1808; the Martin mill, which produced paper by grinding up old rags; Stephen Perley's mill, which produced linseed oil from flax; and a bell foundry begun in 1810. The foundry made sleigh bells, door knockers and big bells for the mills and churches. Meredith Bridge village had a post office by 1805, and the principal citizens founded a social library in 1807—the only one to be established anywhere in the town of Meredith. By 1813, Meredith Bridge had stores, a church (but no minister yet), a school, John Harper's law office, Zadock Bowman's medical practice and lending business and Jonathan Folsom's hotel.[35]

Meredith Bridge grew by leaps and bounds. The Meredith Cotton and Woolen Company, one of the first mills to make woolen goods, was established shortly after 1812. In 1814, citizens concerned about the threat of fire in the village's wood-frame buildings organized the Meredith Bridge Hose Company. An academy was founded in 1820 and the Meredith Bridge Savings Bank in

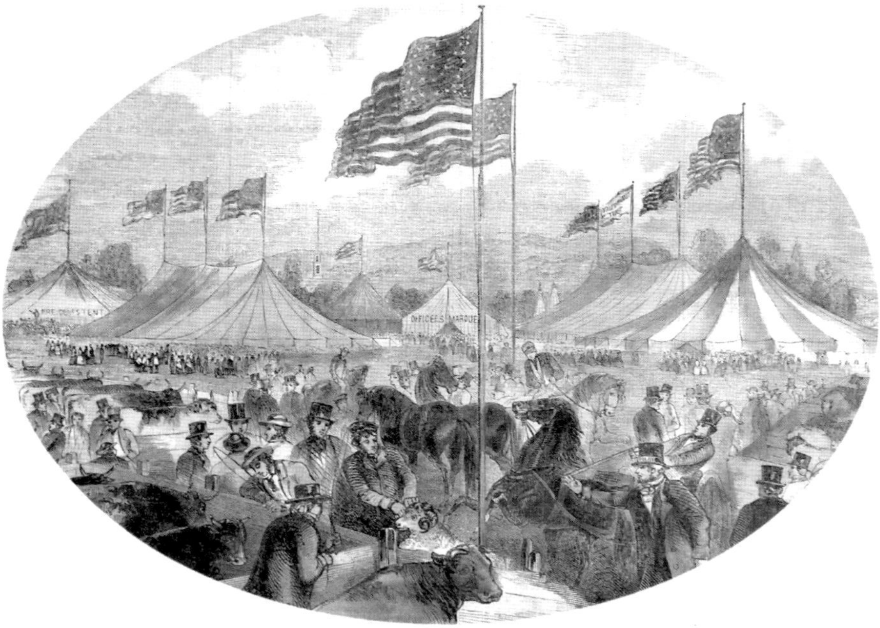

The New Hampshire State Fair at Meredith Bridge, 1852. *From* Gleason's Pictorial.

1831. By the 1840s, the first hosiery knitting mills had been built, and there was a newspaper (the *Belknap Gazette*) and a printing shop and bookbindery. The village had three cotton mills, a shingle and clapboard mill, a sash and door machinery mill, a tannery, ten stores, two druggists, a jeweler and watchmaker, two barbers, five lawyers, three taverns and three churches. There was also a campaign for civic improvement: in 1842, the Meredith Bridge Washingtonian Total Abstinence Association, with Harriet Gale as secretary, convinced the tavern owners to stop serving liquor.[36]

In Meredith Center, there was a single dam across Mill Brook, with the mills clustered there. After the early gristmill and sawmill, a wool carding and fulling mill was built in about 1820. That mill probably increased its business as the sheep boom grew on surrounding farms from 1820 to 1840. According to Maud Rollins, the finishing of linen cloth and the pressing of clothes were also done in this or an adjoining mill.[37]

On Meredith Bay, Meredith Village had a sawmill, a gristmill and a fulling mill in 1810, and in 1822, it had five stores, a tannery, a cloth dressing and manufacturing company, three lawyers and one doctor.[38] A post office was established in 1820 and rotated among the stores according to the political affiliation of the store owner, who was appointed postmaster by the U.S. president.

The water power resource in Meredith Village was given a big boost in 1818 by resident and store owner John Bond Swasey. Born in 1782, John was the son of early Meredith settlers Benjamin and Jane (Bond) Swasey. After Benjamin's death in 1783, Jane married Stephen Adams, and John grew up in that household with six brothers and sisters. In 1809, he married Alice Ladd, and together they would raise five children in their home on Main Street. John owned a general store in Meredith and was the village's third postmaster.

At that time, Meredith village's original mills were located along Measley Pond Brook, which ran from an "upper dam" at Measley Pond (Lake Waukewan) down to Lake Winnipesaukee. Along this brook (and using its water power) were a sawmill, a gristmill and a fulling mill. Northeast of this natural outlet of Lake Waukewan was a long cove extending east toward the village. John Swasey owned land between the cove and the village, but others owned the land and the mills along Measley Pond Brook. Perhaps around 1809, Swasey conceived of cutting a canal from the cove, through the village, to create a new and more concentrated source of water power. The single fall of water thus created between Lakes Waukewan and Winnipesaukee would support bigger and better mills.

To accomplish this project, Swasey first had to buy up the Measley Pond Brook land, the mills and, most importantly, the "mill privileges" that allowed the use of the water for power. He began this in 1809, buying land on the south side of the brook from Daniel Avery. In 1811, he bought more land along the brook, including the gristmill and fulling mill, with all their equipment. Also in that year, with Avery's help, Swasey bought the sawmill and mill yard property from a group of six shareholders. In 1813, he purchased two more properties, and in 1816, he bought the remaining piece that Daniel Avery owned. This part of the project took seven years and cost him $5,900 for property purchases.[39]

From 1816 to 1818, he had a new rock-lined canal dug from the cove on Lake Waukewan through Meredith Village to the "head" at today's Mill Falls—a total drop of some forty feet. Here, John Swasey installed new saw, grist, fulling and carding mills. The year 1816 was the "year without a summer," so the six-hundred-foot-long canal project proceeded through that year's cold and inclement weather. In 1828, John and Alice began building a new home on the west side of Main Street, but John died of appendicitis before it was finished. Alice oversaw the finishing of the house and, in a

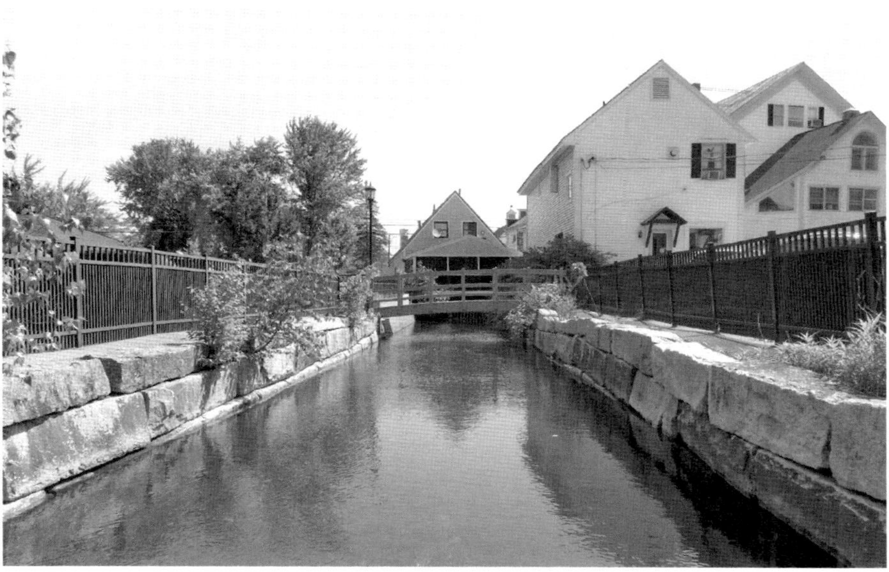

The stone-lined Waukewan Canal goes under buildings and under Meredith village's Main Street, emerging at Mill Falls. *Daniel Heyduk.*

bold move for that time, also oversaw the mills. The water power resource created by John Swasey would continue to serve the village for more than one hundred years.

Families of the late eighteenth and early nineteenth centuries were large, and farming was the principal occupation. Among the young people of each generation, there was a demand for new farmland, and this drove the settlement of Meredith and the surrounding Lakes Region towns. In the first federal census of 1790, Meredith had 881 people, but the population almost doubled in just the next decade and continued upward until it reached 3,351 in 1840. Farms were being established throughout the town, and there were many small sawmills and other water-powered shops on streams in rural localities. Farm families lived on back roads and, depending on transportation by horses and oxen, could not go far from home to trade, order equipment or get it repaired, get the mail or attend church. Locations where mills had been built became natural service centers. Meredith Bridge in the south, Meredith Center in the west, Meredith Village in the north and Center Harbor Village in the east (then partly in the town of Meredith) each grew to provide services to its surrounding rural area.

Meredith Center, for example, had four blacksmith shops, two carpentry shops, two wheelwright/carriage shops, two stores, two schools, a shoemaker, a doctor, a church with parsonage and an inn/stagecoach stop during the 1850s. In Meredith Village at the same time (1859), one could consult a lawyer, visit a "Daguerrean Artist" (photographer), buy footwear at four different stores, buy books and stationery or buy a carriage where they were made. Carpeting and clothing were available at two stores and dry goods and groceries at four. There was a railroad station and express office, stagecoach service, a hotel, a livery stable, a post office and a school. Hats, caps and furs were sold, as were hardware, paints and oils. Meredith Village had three doctors and two drugstores, a lumber dealer and manufacturers of melodeons, pianofortes, stoves, tin and copper ware and rakes.[40] There were the mills at late John Swasey's water power site, now controlled by the Meredith Mechanic Association. Carpenters, shoemakers, blacksmiths, painters, tailors, dressmakers and other tradespeople offered their services.

In the early 1860s, according to Edgar Maloon, the water power for a newly built mill was still obtained from a traditional overshot waterwheel, which turned vertically as the water poured down on it. Maloon's description

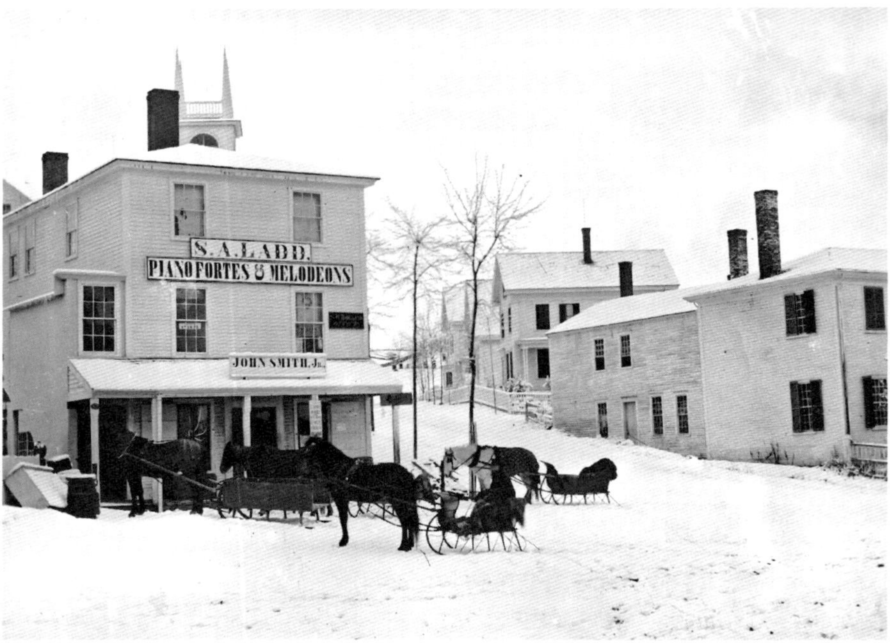

The current Historical Society Museum was Seneca Ladd's pianoforte and melodeon manufacturing business. *Meredith Historical Society.*

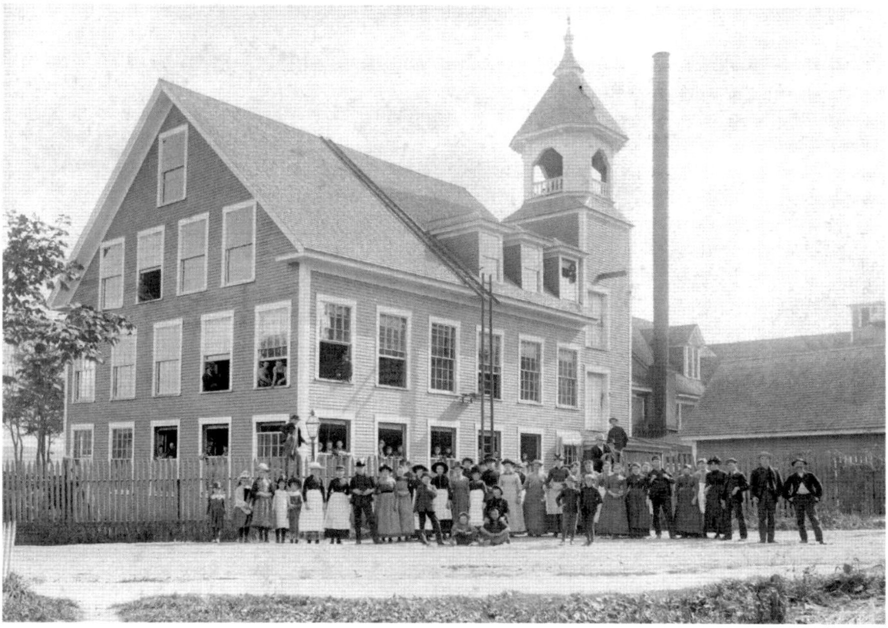

The Hodgson Hosiery Mill, 1880s. *Meredith Historical Society.*

of how this Meredith Village cotton stocking mill operated gives an idea of the prodigious water power that John Swasey had created. The cotton was unbaled and fed into a rotating "willowing" machine and then into a "picking" machine, which spread the cotton fibers into sheets. The sheets went to a carding machine and were carried by a continuous belt to several rolling machines, which prepared them for the spinner. The spinning machine made the cotton into thread; now on bobbins, it went to the knitting machine. The knit cotton was then hand cut and machine stitched into a stocking. The stockings were "finished" by being washed in a revolving tub that had power-driven paddles, or hammers; then they were steamed, rinsed in a surge of water and dried in "a wire cylinder that whirled at great speed." The stockings were next bleached in chloride of lime and oil of vitriol, re-rinsed and dried again in a whirling cylinder. Power pressing followed and then finally stamping, folding and boxing for shipment to New York City.[41] The number of machines in just this one of several mills indicates the water power that was available via the Waukewan Canal. That power was later used by the Hodgson Hosiery Mill, the Meredith Linen Mill and the Meredith Electric Light Company, which supplied electricity to the village.

The Boston, Concord & Montreal Railroad was built to Meredith Bridge in 1848 and then to Lakeport and the Weirs. By that time, Meredith Bridge had many mills and machine shops, while Lakeport had mills, machine shops and boat building. The Weirs was undeveloped, but it crucially had convenient access to Lake Winnipesaukee for a steamboat transportation link. These places also were located on the easiest and cheapest gradient for building the railroad bed and laying tracks.

The Waukewan Canal's bountiful and concentrated water power had given Meredith Village a boost toward manufacturing. Meredith Village's location on the lakeshore also offered a continuous easy gradient for building a roadbed from the Weirs. The railroad was extended along the Winnipesaukee shore to Meredith Village in 1849 and then along the Waukewan and Winona lakeshores to Ashland, which was another growing mill center. The rails bypassed Meredith Center, where the mills, stores and tradesmen primarily served the surrounding farms. Center Harbor Village in east Meredith did not get the railroad either, but it was to benefit as a prime destination in summer steamboat service on Lake Winnipesaukee, fed by lakeside railroad connections at the Weirs and at Alton Bay.

In the 1850s, Meredith Bridge was growing fast, Meredith Village more slowly and Meredith Center not at all. Meredith town meetings had been held for years at the old meetinghouse on Parade Road, but nothing else was there, and Meredith Neck people resented the long trip. In 1854, it was voted to build a new meetinghouse in Meredith Village that would be more convenient for people on Meredith Neck but less so for the growing population in Meredith Bridge. The building was still unfinished when the March 1855 town meeting was held there, reportedly attended by some eight hundred people. Their combined weight caused the floor to collapse. Sixty were seriously injured, four died and many were permanently disabled. Shocked by the catastrophe and already pursuing their own fortunes, the residents of Meredith Bridge asked the state legislature for division of the town. That was granted in July, creating the new town of Laconia, with Lakeport and the Weirs, and the name "Meredith Bridge" passed into history.

Chapter 9

Painting the Glory of Lakes and Mountains

The Lakes Region was part of the beginning of landscape painting in the United States, attracting some of the first and many of the most famous painters of American scenery. They were among our first tourists, and their work prompted thousands of other tourists to follow in their footsteps.

Until the 1820s, the only painters traveling around the region were portrait painters, who would arrive in a town, advertise their availability for a week or a month, paint likenesses of members of prominent families and then repeat the process in another town. In the summer of 1827, a solitary and different painter, Thomas Cole, visited Lake Winnipesaukee and the White Mountains. Cole was interested in painting scenery, and he did it extraordinarily well. From a sketch he made on Lake Winnipesaukee, he created a painting of the lake that was exhibited at the National Academy of Design. The painting shows the lake in its wild state, with a lone sail (a gundalow?) to indicate human presence. In the foreground is a traveler resting beside a rough road at the base of a huge rock, capped by a gnarled tree. Around the lake are mountains much craggier and steeper than those Cole actually saw. The technique worked. A wealthy patron bought the painting, and an engraving was made and published in the *American Landscape* by William Cullen Bryant in 1830. From his 1827 and 1828 trips, Cole also produced a sketch from Red Hill and paintings of Mount Chocorua, Crawford Notch and Mount Washington.[42]

Thomas Cole produced a second painting of Lake Winnipesaukee in 1828. Titled *View on Lake Winnipiseogee*, this painting was done from a

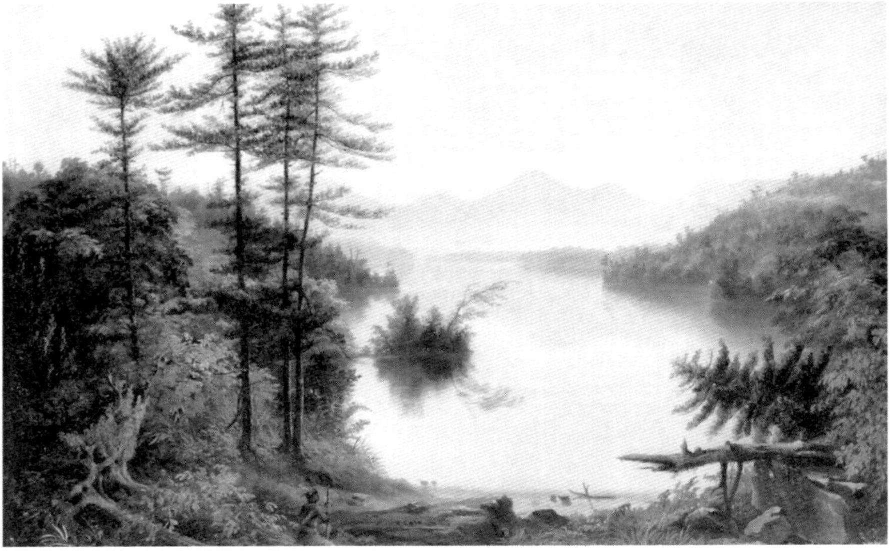

View on Lake Winnipiseogee, Thomas Cole's 1828 painting of Meredith Bay as seen from today's Scenic Park. *Wadsworth Atheneum Museum of Art, Hartford, Connecticut.*

sketch made by his patron, Daniel Wadsworth. Wadsworth had sketched the view down Meredith Bay from the shore at present Scenic Park, showing the Belknap Mountains in the distance. Writing to Wadsworth about the painting he had created, Cole said, "I have imagined it in its wild state—it is a morning view in Indian Summer." Perhaps because Wadsworth's sketch was not exaggerated, the painting is quite accurate—a view looking south from present-day Meredith as Native Americans would have seen it.

In the 1830s, well-known professional artist William Henry Bartlett visited from England and stayed to sketch a *View of Meredith* looking north from Ladd Hill. The view shows the village as it was then and Meredith Bay, with the Congregational Church in its former location near the shore on today's Pleasant Street. Bartlett also sketched Center Harbor and Center Harbor Bay from Sunset Hill, including the then-Meredith shoreline. His sketches were printed as engravings in the popular 1840 book *American Scenery*, which had a wide circulation in Europe and America.

Thomas Cole's focus on landscape, emphasizing its wildness and grandeur, influenced other artists, and their work came to be called the "Hudson River School" or the "White Mountain School" of American art. At that time, prominent Americans bought paintings and supported artists. Popular paintings were quickly issued as prints and bought by people of more average means. Among artists capturing scenes around Meredith were Russell Smith (*Lake Winnipiseogee*), Samuel Lancaster Gerry (*Road in East Meredith*) and Robert Wilkie (*Moonlight on Lake Winnipiseogee*). Samuel Gerry and Ferdinand Richardt each painted Center Harbor Bay from Garnet Hill, then in Meredith. Beginning in the 1840s, artists became captivated by the pastoral landscape of the Lakes Region at that time. They roamed over the countryside, capturing the scenery in a new realistic style. Their landscapes featured the tamed and cultivated land, farm animals and picturesque buildings and villages set against the backdrop of the still wild-appearing mountains. These paintings accurately show the landscape of the town as it then was. Between the 1830s and 1900, artists trooped to the Lakes Region and the White Mountains, prompting local people to open their homes as boardinghouses. Hundreds of prominent artists painted the scenery, producing almost ninety notable paintings of Lake Winnipesaukee alone.[43]

At the same time, writers were describing the scenery and making nature—especially wild nature—a subject of national fascination. Captivated by the idea of "sublime" scenery, tourists began to come to see it for themselves. Boardinghouses multiplied and hotels appeared. Some hotels enticed "resident" artists by offering them discounted room and board. Other guests could watch them paint, and many of the resulting paintings had the hotels in them as free—and very effective—advertising. The popularized scenery of lakes, mountains, farms and villages drew tourists, who needed transportation, accommodation, guidebooks, guides and souvenirs to take home.

In the years before the Civil War, guidebooks began to appear to help travelers take it all in. The most elaborate of these was Thomas Starr King's *The White Hills: Their Legends, Landscapes, and Poetry*, first published in 1859. In addition to describing the mountains, Starr King portrayed Lake Winnipesaukee in rapturous words that enticed nineteenth-century travelers. Describing travel by steamer in the "Lake Winnipiseogee" chapter, he wrote:

> *As we shoot out into the breadth of the lake, and take in the wide scene, there is no ripple on its bosom. The little islands float over liquid silver, and glide by each other silently, as in the movements of a dance, while our boat changes her heading. And all around, the mountains, swelling softly, or cutting the sky with jagged lines of steely blue, vie with the molten mirror at our feet for the privilege of holding the eye. The "sun-sparks" blaze thick as stars upon the glassy wrinkles of the water.*

Turning to practical matters, he related that "steamers ply from the railroad stations at Alton Bay and Weir's, several times in the day. Thus, when the weather is pleasant, persons may pass the larger part of the day on the lake, and may take their meals on the boat if they choose." He urged readers to see the lake from as many vantage points as possible and to note even the shapes of the pines along the shore. Other guidebooks dutifully discussed trains, hotels and stagecoaches, but Starr King's was landscape painting in words.

Chapter 10

THE GREAT SHEEP BOOM AND AFTER

Meredith's early settlers had a small number of hardy sheep to provide meat and a coarse grade of wool for home spinning and weaving, and for many years, that was all they needed. Merino sheep in Spain had very fine wool, but the Spanish government forbade the export of Merinos in order to keep a national monopoly. Then, Napoleon Bonaparte invaded Spain, and in 1809, the Spanish gave American diplomat William Jarvis the chance to buy thousands of sheep and ship them to the United States. At the same time, trouble between the United States and the British led first to trade problems and then to the War of 1812. Suddenly, New Englanders had the finest wool-producing sheep in the world and an urgent need to produce their own cloth. Woolen cloth, blanket and carpet mills sprung up throughout New England. Farmers acquired the new sheep and cleared more and more forest for pasture. Steadily increasing prices for wool fed the boom.

There are about 6,500 sheep in New Hampshire today, but near the height of the sheep boom in 1836, there were 465,000. Meredith had 3,826 sheep in 1840, more sheep than its 3,351 people. Among New Hampshire towns, that was just average. Walpole had some 15,000 sheep in one year. There were more than one hundred woolen factories in the state at that time, and demand for wool was increasing.[44] Sheep require extensive but not particularly rich pasture, and farmers cleared ever more forest to graze ever more sheep. It seemed the perfect economic use for thin-soiled, rocky hillsides. Many of the stone walls now found in the forest high on Meredith's hills date from that time of maximum clearing of the land.

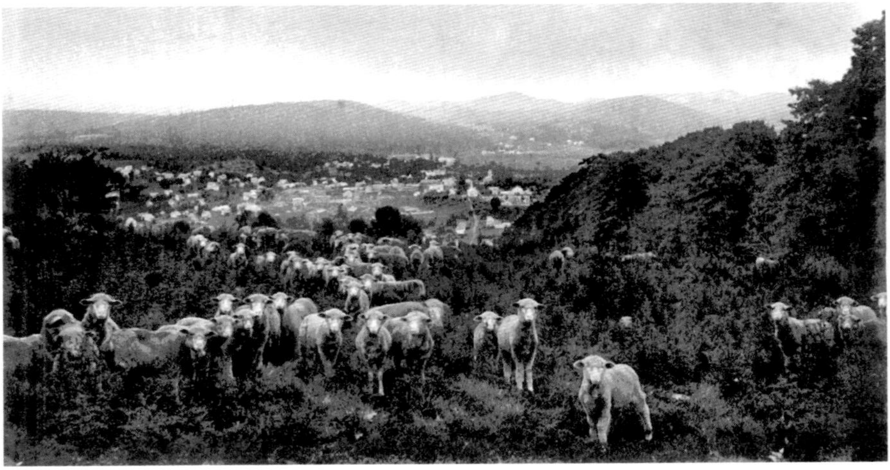

Sheep seemed ideal for rocky pastures cleared from forest on the high slopes. *New Hampshire Historical Society.*

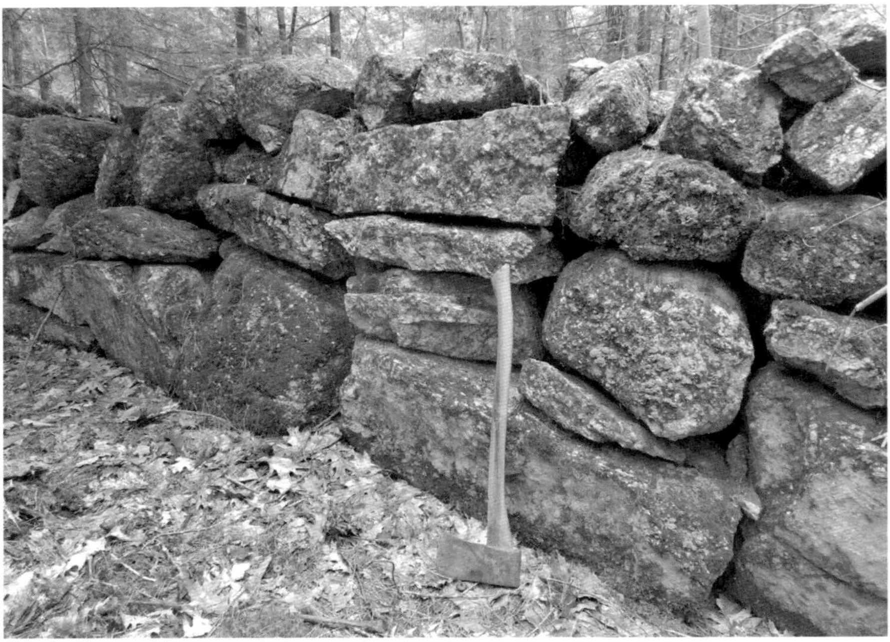

Walls enclosing sheep pasture were high and built of large stones. *Daniel Heyduk.*

Not only did farmers have to clear much new pasture and build walls to enclose it, but they also had to build sheds to shelter the sheep indoors from November to April and grow much more hay, oats and corn to feed them. Sheep required salt once a week and had to be treated for various diseases. If these things were neglected, the quality of the wool would be affected. Finally, the sheep were shorn, and the wool was washed and sold to textile mills in Laconia, Northfield, Franklin, Campton, Holderness, Bristol and Rochester.

Sheep were big business while the boom lasted, but by the 1840s, wool from western farms had entered the market via expanding railroads and the Erie Canal. Even as early as 1836, Ohio had more than 1.7 million sheep, which cost the midwestern farmer only twenty-five cents to a dollar per head per year, compared to one to two dollars per head for the New England farmer. At the same time, wool prices dropped from fifty-eight cents per pound in 1836 to twenty-five cents per pound by the late 1840s.[45] Town tax records show farms with fewer sheep each year, leading to abandonment of pasture and return of the forest. Some farmers continued to raise sheep as breeding stock or for the meat market, and the Civil War created an increased demand for wool for military uniforms and blankets. By the end of the war in 1865, however, the sheep boom had ended.

At that time, too, more New Englanders were working in factories or moving to the west, enticed there by railroad land offers and letters from relatives extolling the advantages of western farming. Meredith's population (without Laconia) went from 1,944 people in 1860 to 1,638 in 1910, with a proportionally greater drop in the farm population than in the village population. Farming at that time was still labor intensive, and fewer people on farms meant lower production and less income. Luckily, Meredith was experiencing an influx of summer vacation visitors, drawn by the scenery, guidebook descriptions, the health benefits of rural life and railroad advertising. Some farms were able to attract summer vacationers by offering room and board, together with a quiet country setting and recreational opportunities.

Beginning in the late 1840s, just when sheep were on the wane, tourist guidebooks began to appear. One of the earliest was *Tripp's White Mountain Guide Book; or, Guide to the Mountain and Lake Scenery of New Hampshire.* This guide was updated every two or three years and described points of interest along the main travel corridors, including the Boston, Concord and Montreal rail line through Meredith and steamer service on Lake Winnipesaukee. The flow of summer visitors continued each year through the nineteenth century and into the twentieth, and many tourists returned to the same hotel or boardinghouse each summer.

For visitors making their first summer vacation visit to Meredith in 1902, it would have been very helpful for them to use *The Tourists' Guide-Book to the State of New Hampshire*, published by Frank West Rollins. This book gave a brief history of the town, together with information about transportation, communications, churches, places to stay and things to do. The automobile era had not yet begun in 1902, so a family's trip would not be much different from one in 1892 or 1882. They would use the railroad, steamboats, stagecoaches and horse-drawn wagons and would stay for some time at their lodging, enjoying what it had to offer and making the acquaintance of their hosts and the other guests.

Meredith's Boston & Maine Railroad station would be the point of arrival, located on the land where the lumberyard is today. They would be met at the station by a coach or horse and wagon sent to convey them and their baggage to the hotel or boardinghouse. In 1902, there were twelve trains per day passing through Meredith—six northbound and six southbound. The 7:26 a.m. train brought the day's Boston and other newspapers. The town of 1,713 people (more than 6,000 today) had both telegraph and telephone service. None of the village streets was paved, although Meredith was a bustling mill town with many workers living in apartments and boardinghouses in the village center. There were many stores, blacksmith shops and a new brick library but no hotel. If the visitors wanted to stay in the village, the descriptions of two of the tourist boardinghouses might have looked attractive. The Maples was owned by A.S. Clough, accommodated twenty guests and cost $1.00 per day, or $5.00 to $7.00 per week. The *Guide* noted that "this house is on high ground; city water; shade in front, pastures in rear. Near Lakes Winnipiseogee and Waukewan, thirty rods [five hundred feet] from post-office [today's historical society building]." Another, the Waukewan House, owned by W.E.S. Foss, accommodated twenty-five guests at $1.50 per day or $7.00 to $10.00 per week. The *Guide* noted that it was "within 5 minutes' walk from Lake Waukewan and Winnipiseogee, station and post-office. Good black bass and lake trout fishing. Large, pleasant rooms."

There were also options outside Meredith Village. One was Elmwood House, owned by Austin S. Moulton and accommodating twenty guests at one dollar per day or five dollars per week (today's Moulton farm). The *Guide* tells us that Elmwood "is situated near Lake Winnipiseogee; it is simply a farmhouse which has been open for boarders nine seasons." The listing for Mountain View, owned by W.H. Keyser, was much more enticing. It noted that

> *this house is one mile from village and three miles from Centre Harbor, on main road. High location; has a large piazza* [porch] *surrounded by noble elms with views that are unsurpassed, making it one of the finest locations*

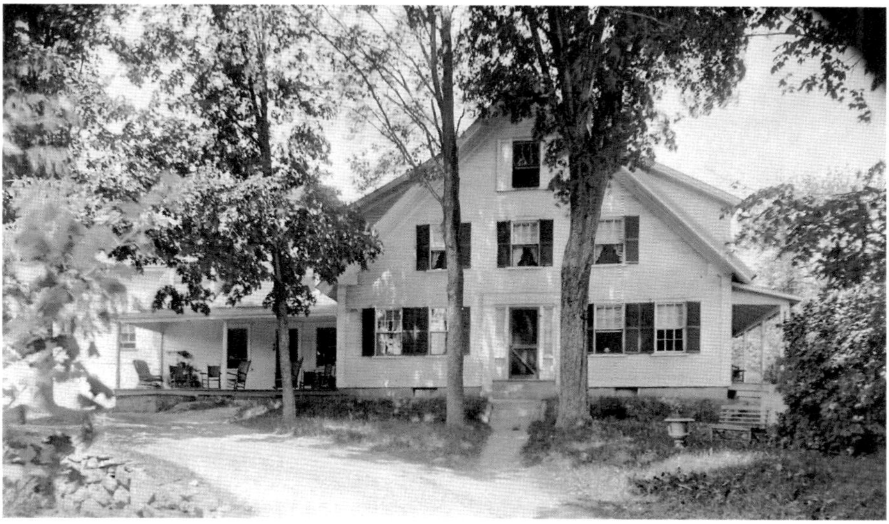

The Maples, a tourist boardinghouse in Meredith Village. *Meredith Historical Society.*

> *in the state. The rooms are large and airy with two beds in each, just the thing for families or parties. A good table, good substantial food, plenty of milk, cream and vegetables off the farm. The house has a fine piano. A nice mountain team will take parties to places of interest at reasonable rates.*

This house accommodated thirty guests at one dollar per day or five to seven dollars per week.

A family with small children might decide to stay at Elmwood House, despite its very modest write-up. First, they could see that the descriptions in the guide were written by the boardinghouse owners themselves, and Austin Moulton was not being promotional. Second, the Moulton family—Austin and Laura Ann along with their children, Nathan and Alice—were well known in Meredith, where he had served as selectman. Third, the Moultons had room for children, having constructed small cubicles where they could sleep separate from their parents. Finally, the Moulton farmhouse was off the main road, where it was safer for children to play. Guests at the farm probably enjoyed Page Pond, just to the south on Quarry Road.

Austin and Laura Moulton had been running their farm since the early 1880s. During the 1890s and early 1900s, the Moulton farm had two to three horses, three to nine cows and fifteen to twenty sheep but no oxen. These may have been rented or borrowed as needed from their Quarry

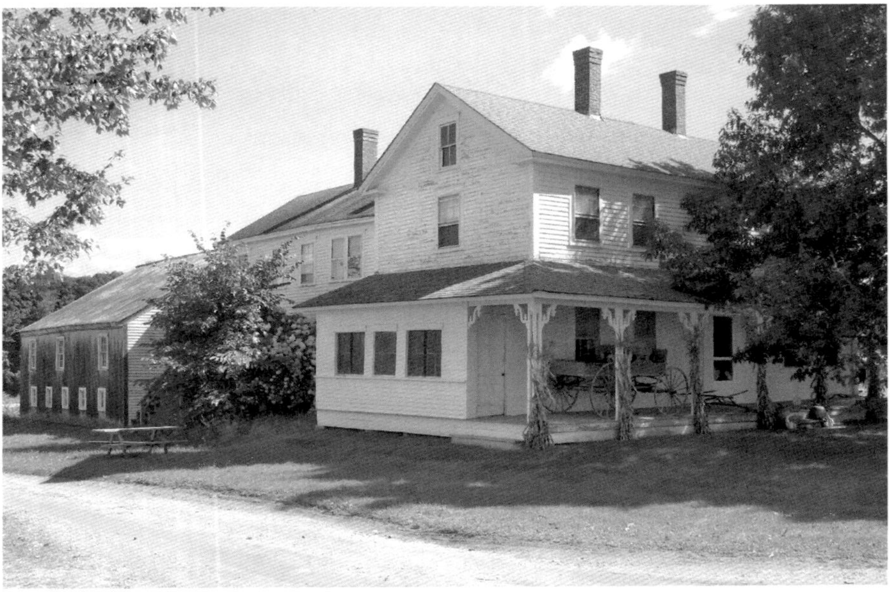

Elmwood House, owned in 1902 by Austin and Laura Ann Moulton, is today's Moulton Farm. *Daniel Heyduk.*

Road neighbors, the Leavitts, who had as many as seven oxen in 1903. The Moultons' successful business strategy included dairy farming, stock raising and accommodating vacationing summer boarders. In addition to those mentioned, Rollins's *Tourists' Guide-Book* listed eight more tourist boardinghouses in Meredith in 1902.

In 1915, the New Hampshire Board of Agriculture's glossy booklet *New Hampshire Farms for Summer Homes* reported that boarders would pay seven to fifteen dollars per week and that when the farmer could raise his own vegetables, milk, cream, butter and eggs, his profit would be the greatest. A farm that hosted boarders for the summer might earn more income in that time than the farm alone could earn in the whole year. Of course, the burden fell heavily on the housekeepers. The board's booklet did mention that "the wife and children sometimes find the employment exacting and tiresome."

Chapter 11

The Boston, Concord & Montreal and the Boston & Maine Railroads

The story of Lakes Region railroad service begins in Lowell, Massachusetts. Railroads were being chartered and track laid in the 1830s, and one of the first lines ran between Boston and the textile mill center at Lowell. This was originally envisioned as a freight line to serve the mills and actually bypassed many towns along the way. However, the people of Lowell loved the idea of riding to Boston at the unheard-of speed of forty miles per hour, and the Boston & Lowell Railroad discovered that passengers were as profitable as freight. Meanwhile, the textile industry quickly expanded up the Merrimack River to the growing towns of Nashua, Merrimack, Manchester and Concord, and the need for a railroad connection led to the chartering of the Nashua & Lowell and the Concord Railroads in 1835. Rail service reached Concord in 1842 and proved highly profitable right from the start. So, yet another railroad, the Boston, Concord & Montreal (BC&M), was chartered in 1844, with a route to run from Concord to Plymouth and on to Wells River, Vermont. However, investors were beginning to look west, there was competition from railroads in the Connecticut Valley and there were fewer mills along the intended BC&M route, so financing proved difficult. Construction did not start until 1846, and the treasurer reported that "the stockholders in our road are nearly all residents of the country." Lakes Region investors and towns had bought a substantial stake in their hoped-for rail connection to Concord and beyond.

The line was built eighteen miles through Northfield and Sanbornton Bridge (Tilton) to Meredith Bridge (Laconia) by 1848. The first train to arrive there was pulled by the locomotive "Old Man of the Mountains," and both engine and cars were painted a fresh sky blue. The beginning of service was marked by the firing of a cannon and the ringing of mill and church bells. Rails were then extended through Lakeport, where rail yards and sheds would be built, across Paugus Bay and on to Weirs station. Here a connection with the BC&M-owned steamer *Lady of the Lake* made the BC&M "first on the lake" with combined rail and steamboat service to Center Harbor and Wolfeboro. The Winnipesaukee lakeshore was the route to Meredith, ten miles from Laconia, where a turntable and small engine house were built. Service had reached Ashland and Plymouth by 1850. The BC&M initially owned four engines, six passenger coaches, three baggage cars and fifty freight cars. Passenger coaches were lit by whale oil lamps and heated by stoves. The line was extended to Rumney and Warren by 1851, on to Haverhill and finally across the Connecticut River to Wells River, Vermont, in 1853. Coal was expensive this far north, so the BC&M was a wood-burning railroad, using some thirty thousand cords per year, with Warren as its main wood yard. The high point in service was about 1890, when ten passenger trains per day were running between Concord and Wells River junction.[46]

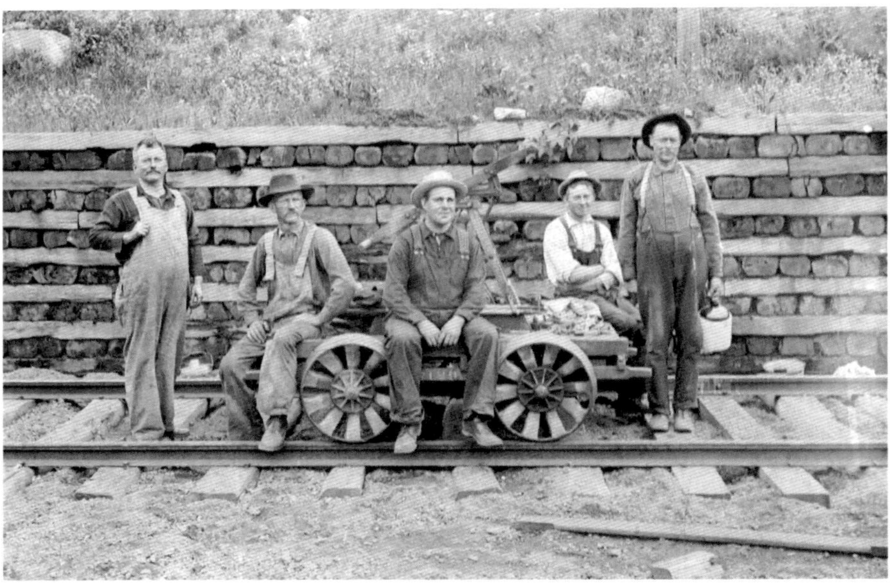

A Boston & Maine Railroad section crew, 1912. *Meredith Historical Society.*

Accidents involving trains happened every year, but the BC&M's greatest tragedy occurred in 1854. A special passenger train was being run from the state fair in Laconia north to Meredith and Plymouth. To avoid paying the fare, some young men jumped onto the engine's front running boards. The conductor had the train stopped on the Paugus Bay trestle and went up to collect their fares. At that moment, the regular northbound passenger train rounded the curve onto the trestle and smashed into the rear of the special. Six people were killed and forty badly hurt.

On a happier note, the BC&M excelled as a tourist railroad to the Lakes Region and White Mountains, using connections via the *Lady of the Lake*, a branch line from Plymouth to Lincoln and stagecoach service at Meredith Village, Littleton and Whitefield.

Tourism and competition in the transportation market between 1850 and the early twentieth century produced the golden age of railroads and steamboats on Lake Winnipesaukee. The almost simultaneous arrival of two rail lines at the lake—the Boston, Concord & Montreal at Lakeport and the Weirs in 1848–49 and the Cocheco Railroad at Alton in 1851—added a new competitive steamboat dimension.

In Lakeport, a group of investors had formed the Winnipesaukee Steamboat Company and built the innovative, 125-foot side-wheel steamer *Lady of the Lake*. At its successful launch in 1849, the *Lady* was by far the largest and fastest boat on the lake. The BC&M owners saw the potential of this boat to control water transportation from all lakeside points to their rail link, and they promptly bought it. The *Lady*—which could carry four hundred passengers, freight and mail—began regular trips between the Weirs station/dock, Center Harbor and Wolfeboro. Tracks of the BC&M went on to Meredith village, so no water link was needed there.

The Cocheco Railroad was nearing Alton Bay, and its owners hastened to build their own steamboat—the one-hundred-foot-long *Dover*. By 1852, the rails had reached the bay, a station and dock were ready and the *Dover* began service between Alton Bay, Wolfeboro, Long Island, Center Harbor and Meredith. (Dover Street in Meredith village goes to the town docks.) The *Dover* was forbidden to dock at the Weirs, and the *Lady* did not go to Alton Bay, but both boats competed for business in Wolfeboro, which would not have a rail link until 1872. The richest prize was Center Harbor, the terminus of overland freight and stage routes from the north and east—all the way from Conway, which did not get rail service until 1872.

Tourists converged on Center Harbor from both the Weirs and Alton, some to stay at the Senter House or other hotels and boardinghouses, some

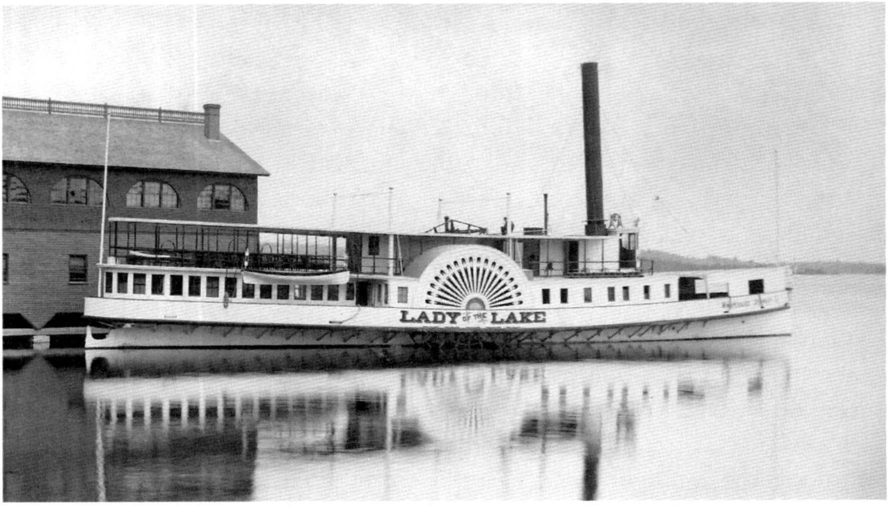

The Boston, Concord & Montreal Railroad's *Lady of the Lake* steamer traveled Lake Winnipesaukee from a dock at the Weirs rail station. *Meredith Historical Society.*

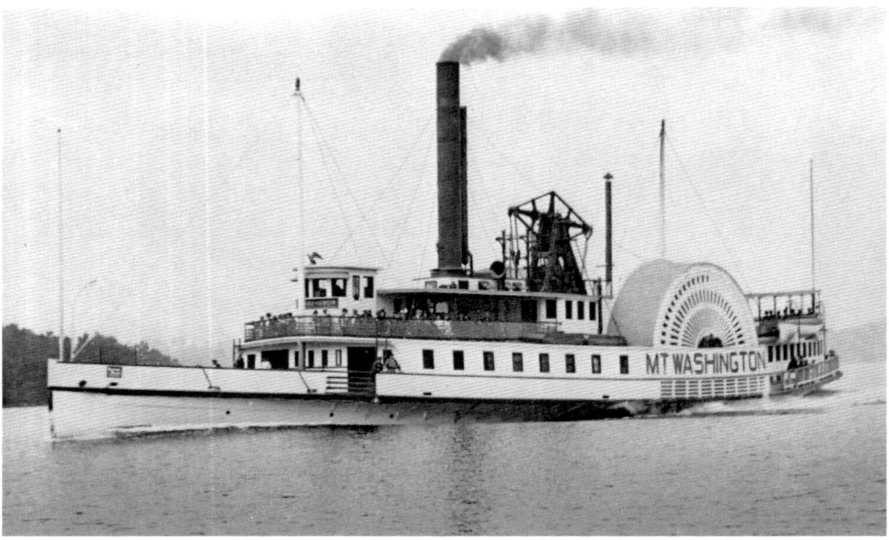

The Boston & Maine Railroad's *Mt Washington* steamer carried mail, passengers and freight on Lake Winnipesaukee from a railhead at Alton Bay. *Meredith Historical Society.*

to go on to Moultonborough or Sandwich and some to take the connecting stage to North Conway and beyond. The competing boats often raced one another, giving the passengers a bonus in addition to the scenery. The *Lady* easily won these races, and the Cocheco Railroad had *Dover* lengthened and rechristened *Chocorua*. Its new boat could carry more but still could not beat the *Lady*.

The Boston & Maine Railroad (B&M) entered the scene in 1863 by leasing the Cocheco system. It decided to build a new, large, fast boat, and the result was the 178-foot side-wheel steamer *Mt Washington*, launched in 1872. The *Lady* and the "*Mount*" competed for eighteen more years, to the delight of all who rode aboard them. The BC&M later became the Concord & Montreal, until it was first leased, and then it was taken over by the B&M in 1895. The end of railroad competition also ended the career of the *Lady of the Lake*. The B&M's *Mt Washington* became Lake Winnipesaukee's only railroad steamer beginning in 1893. From that time, the *Mount* served all lakeside towns except Meredith, because the B&M served Meredith by rail.[47]

The B&M also experienced a tragic wreck. On the night of September 14–15, 1900, two freight trains collided at full speed in a terrible wreck just north of the Weirs station. At that time, Boston & Maine freight trains were controlled by a dispatcher in Woodsville, who telegraphed instructions to stations along the line. Trains would be told to proceed to and stop at a given station, and the conductor on the train would receive further instructions from the station agent when that station was reached. That night, the regular northbound freight left Concord with orders to stop at Lakeport, where it would meet a southbound "extra" freight. The extra was running late, and after reaching Plymouth, it was told to proceed only as far as Meredith. Both trains were held on sidings at those stations to allow the northbound "Montreal Express" to pass through. The dispatcher then telegraphed Meredith and Lakeport to tell the two trains to meet at the Weirs, but after sending that message, he annulled it and sent an order for them to meet at Meredith. The northbound regular freight received that order and started for Meredith, but the southbound extra train received only the annulment of the Weirs order and set off for Lakeport. They were then on a collision course and could be stopped only if the station agent at the Weirs could signal them to do so. Unfortunately, the night agent at the Weirs had been taken off duty at the end of the summer season just the night before, so the only station between Meredith and Lakeport that could signal a train to stop was unattended.

A worker at the Weirs who collected the mailbags left by the "Montreal Express" heard the telegraph key clicking furiously, but he did not understand Morse code. Before he left the station, the northbound freight roared through. Both trains were running at full speed when they collided

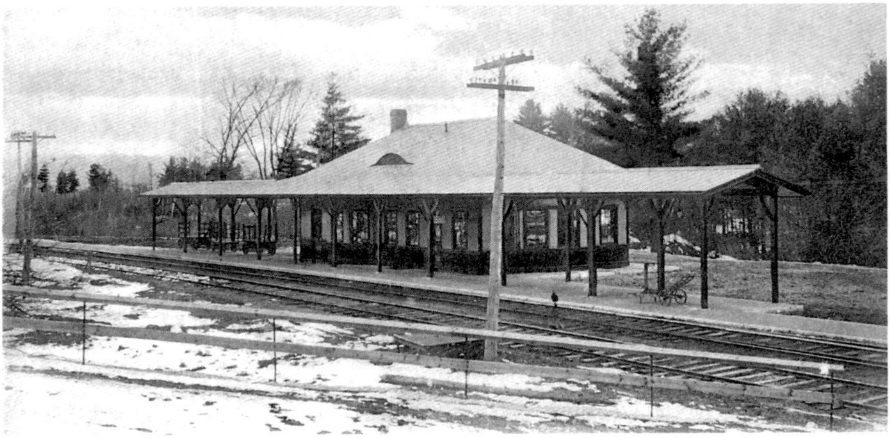

Meredith's railroad station at today's lumberyard once saw twelve trains per day. *Meredith Historical Society.*

at a blind curve just north of the Weirs station. Noise of the impact was heard by a night watchman ten miles away in Center Harbor. The heavy locomotives smashed into each other with such force that they could not be separated later by wrecking crews, and the coal tenders and following freight cars slammed into one another and derailed in a huge pile of twisted wreckage. Splintered wood, twisted iron and the contents of more than forty freight cars made up the rest of the wreck, from which several injured and two dead trainmen were eventually pulled. The casualties came mostly from crew members in the locomotives of the two trains.

Contents of the freight cars—including bananas, potatoes, crates of grapes, fish, lobsters, turkeys, chickens and more—were strewn over the site of the wreck. The B&M made no attempt to salvage the freight, so people came with wheelbarrows and by boat to pick up this bounty and take it home. It took several days to clear the wreck, which was right at the lakeshore, and the night sky was lit by fires that the wrecking crew used to burn debris. The New Hampshire Board of Railroad Commissioners concluded that the wreck was the fault of the trainmen of the extra freight, who left Meredith without a valid order. Under the standing rules, "an extra must keep out of the way of all regular trains."[48]

Chapter 12

MEREDITH LIFE IN THE 1800S

In 1817, following the ruined harvests of 1816 (the "year without a summer"), Sanbornton town clerk Joshua Lane noted conditions that must have applied in Meredith as well. In January, he wrote of the "scarcity of all kinds of produce" and, in March, "still worse for scarcity." By April, he noted, "[P]robably more than half the people out of hay; feed short; many cattle die; great scarcity of all kinds of produce and very dear." On Hezekiah and Polly Smith's farm (now Picnic Rock farm in Meredith), wheat grown in the upper southwest field in 1816 was the only crop to survive. Some or all of it was later stolen from their barn.

Good records exist for the food served to guests in taverns, which was probably the common fare of the time. One report from the 1830s noted that "there are four good meals served every day, viz. breakfast, dinner, tea, and supper, at each of which a profusion of meat is brought to the table." One lodger's breakfast was "a hot beef steak, swimming in grease and onions...followed by fried eggs and bacon," while another reported "rump steaks, fish, eggs and a variety of cakes, with tea or coffee," noting that "pies, puddings and cyder...are found only at the small taverns." Others mention hash, cheese, salt fish, dried beef, bread, pickles and potatoes. Breakfast was generally served between 7:00 a.m. and 9:00 a.m.

Dinner was served around 2:00 p.m. and typically consisted of "broth, with a main dish of an English roast surrounded by potatoes…[with] boiled green peas, on which they put butter or a spicy sauce; then baked or fried eggs, boiled or fried fish, salad which may be thinly sliced cabbage…pastries, sweets…a little fruit, some cheese and a pudding." While dinner was like breakfast, the quantities served were larger.

The same foods served at breakfast or dinner also appeared at supper, but in smaller portions. Supper meats were served cold or quickly heated by frying or broiling. Suppertime was usually between 7:00 p.m. and 9:00 p.m. but was preceded by "tea," which was eaten during the later afternoon. This, too, could include meat but also "cake, pies, cheese, bread and butter, doughnuts, jelly, jam and other sweet preserves."[49]

These descriptions do not note the time of year, and there were variations in the fresh food available seasonally. Out-of-season meats would be pickled, smoked, salt-cured or dried. Beans and peas were dried in large quantities, as were apples and other fruits. Salt fish, salt pork and corned beef were winter staples. The cutting of ice and its storage in icehouses dates from the 1820s and preservation by canning dates from the 1840s.

Alcoholic beverages were commonly drunk with all meals and often in between. Hard cider was a basic tavern offering. Rum or other strong drink was considered necessary for workers, much as coffee is today. Alcohol was a standard accompaniment to all public functions and especially elections, town meetings and militia musters. Visitors to any home, including the local minister, were offered alcoholic drinks as basic hospitality. Travelers usually stopped for a drink at each tavern along their route, and residents usually had a drink while visiting the tavern or village store. Rum was a principal ingredient in many medicines and was also assumed to be necessary for the caregivers.

A social reform movement to favor mildly alcoholic cider, wine and beer over strong alcohol was led in New Hampshire by Reverend Jeremy Belknap. By the 1830s, it was gaining public recognition, and along with the increased popularity of coffee and chocolate, customs regarding alcohol changed substantially. Lifestyles were changing with industrialization, and that, too, had an effect on the scheduling and content of meals and on what and when people drank.

At the Meredith town meeting in 1830, it was voted "that the selectmen be authorized and directed to purchase a farm for the use of Said town, and take a Deed of the same...and that such farm shall not exceed the value of fifteen hundred dollars, and...to proceed and make arrangements to move the poor of the Town of Meredith onto said farm as speedily as circumstances will authorize." The Meredith poor farm was at two locations at different times: Hatch Road and the southern end of Meredith Neck.

Due to the once large Hawkins Brook wetland, where Scenic Park is today, travelers between Meredith Village and Meredith Neck had to take a long way around—up Plymouth Street to the south side of the cemetery and then east on the high ground to True Road and down True and Barnard Ridge Roads to the Neck. Around 1830, the wetland was partly filled to create Winnipesaukee Street, the current Route 25, but the route to the Neck continued to be up the hill behind the cemetery and down Barnard Ridge Road. Meredith Neck farmers petitioned the selectmen to build a more direct, level road from the neck to Winnipesaukee Street, and the selectmen agreed on the condition that the farmers build a bridge across

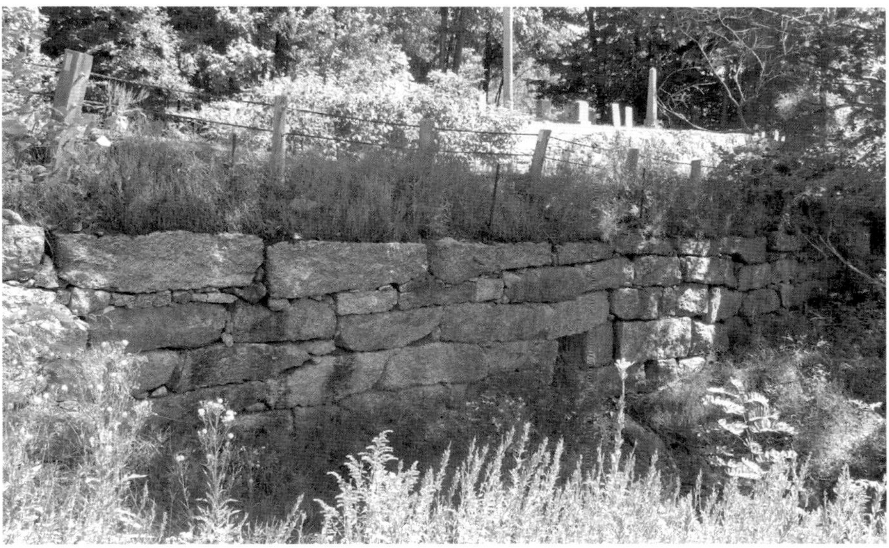

Built by the residents of Meredith Neck before 1833, this bridge still carries traffic on Meredith Neck Road. *Daniel Heyduk.*

Bickford Brook. This brook flowed south through the Smith/Bickford farm and then turned west to cross Meredith Neck Road and empty into Lake Winnipesaukee. There was a ford at that point but no bridge. The farmers built a beautiful, long and substantial bridge of stone blocks that is still there today, near the small cemetery. By contrast, the selectmen changed their minds about building the new direct road. The Meredith Neck farmers appealed to the commissioners of then Strafford County, and in 1833, the commissioners ordered the Meredith selectmen to build the new road, which is today's Pleasant Street.[50]

In March 1845, it was voted "that the selectmen be authorized to invest the sum of $10,000 in the capital stock of the Boston, Concord & Montreal Railroad, providing that the railroad comes through Meredith." As Meredith did not at that time have much industry, the people of Meredith, through their town government, needed to buy stock in order to bring the railroad north.

Recalling a day in 1842, Asa Edgerly of Meredith wrote:

> [W]*hen I was a boy eight years old…I was sent to Sunday School two miles away* [in New Hampton]. *While on the way home…my brother and I fell in with two boys by the name of Carter, who were three or four years older than we were. I had a nice boy's pocket knife which Levi Carter wanted. He offered me two cents* [which] *was a good deal of money to me in those days and I took the two cents and gave him the knife. When I saw something I wanted to cut, I wanted my knife back* [and] *I offered him my two cents. He refused to trade back; then I began to cry. About that time a neighbor came along and asked me what I was crying about. He passed on and told my father that the Carter boys and I were quarreling. Father asked me about it that night and I told him all about the knife trade. He went to Mr. Carter, father of the boy I had sold the knife to, and he being a good man and deacon of the church said, "The boys have been trading on Sunday, have they?" He called his son*

> *Levi and came to my father's and they came to me and asked me for the two cents and I gave it to him. He handed the knife back to me and said "You must not trade on the Sabbath day."*[51]

Asa Edgerly's parents were David and Sarah Edgerly, who had a farm on Gordon Hill Road in New Hampton and, for a time, on Nedeau Road in Meredith. Levi Carter was the son of Malinda and Levi Carter Sr., who had a farm on Carter Mountain Road in New Hampton. Each boy's family had roots in the original settlement of the land. Asa's father was the son of Samuel Edgerly, who bought an original survey lot in Meredith, cleared a farm and raised a large family. Levi's father was the son of Moses Carter, who had bought part of an original undeveloped lot in New Hampton and made a prosperous farm. Edgerly School Road in Meredith and Carter Mountain in New Hampton were named for these early settlers.

Farms depended on the labor of many children, and Asa and Levi Jr. each had ten brothers and sisters. For three generations, the consistent rules had been hard work, piety, sharing within the family and mutual support among neighbors. Asa recalled that

> *the numerous family of my father made clothing and provisions a serious problem, but we never went to bed hungry and we all had a special suit of clothes for Sunday, because father kept sheep and had the wool carded, and the girls spun the wool into thread and my mother wove it into cloth and dyed it, and father had a tailoress come there once a year and made the goods into clothing, and father had a neighbor cobbler come there and make the leather obtained from the slaughtering of the animals into boots and shoes for the family.*[52]

In the 1850 census, among all the occupations recorded in Meredith, Joseph Plumer's occupation of "hermit" was unique. Although he distrusted people and went to some lengths to avoid public functions, he became widely known and received many visitors, to whom he offered hospitality in his own fashion. Joseph lived in a fifteen-foot-square shingle house of his own building on fifty acres that he owned in western Meredith, well distant from the nearest road. The foundation survives today, as does the sill of a barn.

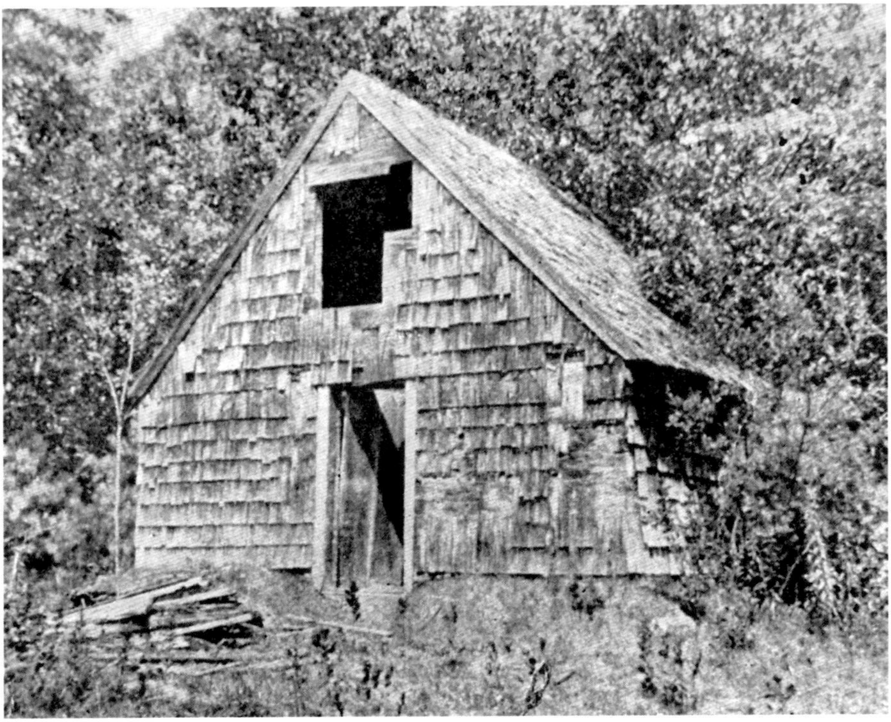

Meredith hermit Joseph Plumer built and lived in this house in today's Hermit Woods Town Forest. *Evelyn Auger.*

Joseph had an orchard and several acres of cleared land, some enclosed with a stone wall. He grew potatoes, corn, vegetables and herbs; he hunted and fished; and he collected many wild edibles. He kept one steer, which pulled his plow and cart, but when this animal died, he designed a cart he could pull himself. The annual yield of Joseph's apple orchard was said to be about seventy-five bushels, and his cider was reputed to be very good.

Joseph was an accomplished craftsman and used a foot-powered lathe to make wooden items for sale, including violins and bass viols. Tapping his maples, Joseph made very dark maple sugar. He also grew tobacco and made snuff. A prominent feature of the homestead was a large scale suspended from a beam in which visitors could be weighed for a penny. Visitors did come—out of curiosity and to buy his wooden wares, maple sugar and snuff. Members of the Plumer family visited him, and his place was a popular destination for young people, including students from the New Hampton Literary and Biblical Institution (now the New Hampton

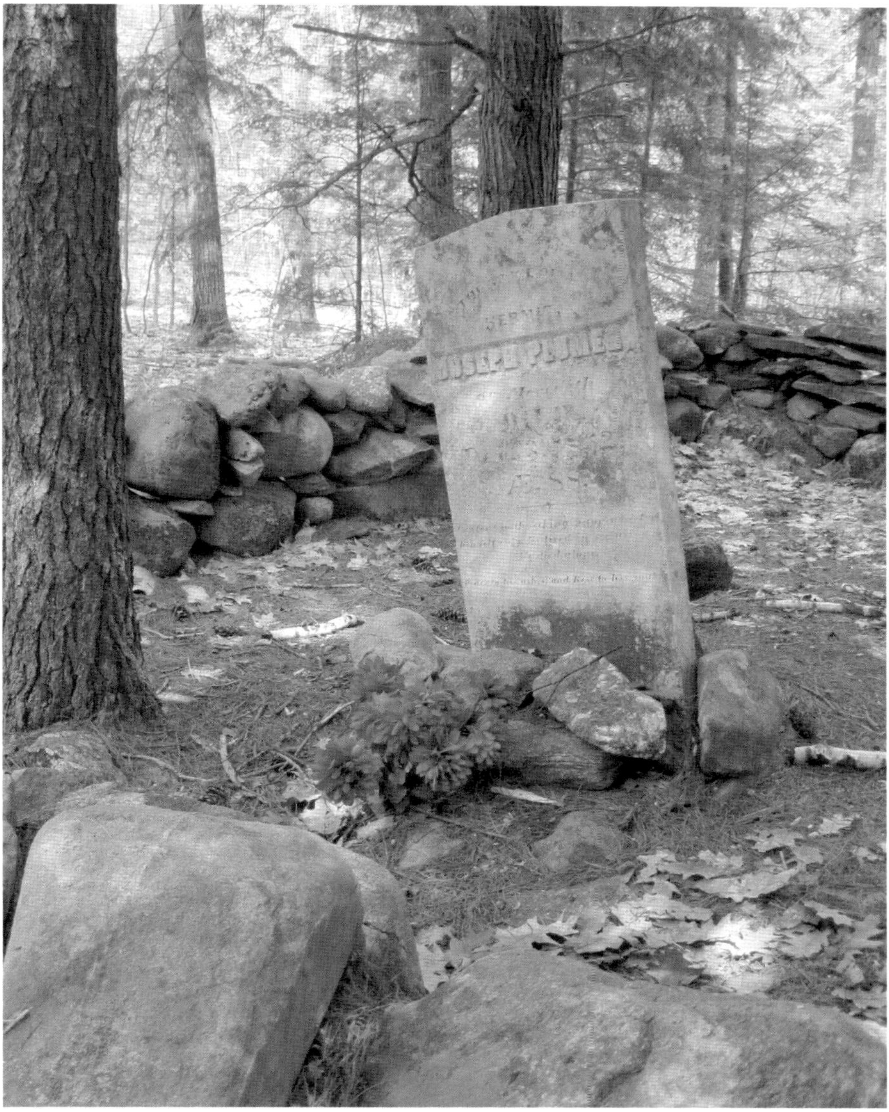

Joseph Plumer's solitary headstone in the walled cemetery he enclosed himself. *Daniel Heyduk.*

School), who discussed Bible subjects with him. Stories suggest that during the warmer months, the "hermit" received many more visits than did the average rural farm. He is said to have offered his visitors apples and cider.

From the business conducted at his homestead, Joseph accumulated a quantity of hard money, which he hid in various locations in his house. He was probably New Hampshire's most financially successful hermit. Joseph was largely self-sufficient and treated his occasional ills with a wide variety of roots and herbs. He was in good health most of his life and outlived all his brothers and sisters. In his later years, a nephew looked in on him regularly. It was during one of those visits, on December 3, 1862, that he was found to have died in his bed at age eighty-eight. The heading on his gravestone reads, "The Grave of a Hermit," and Joseph had indeed lived alone and avoided public gatherings. He is buried not far from where his house stood, at a spot he had selected and enclosed with a stone wall, on land that is now a Meredith town forest on "Hermit Woods Road."[53]

E.H. Maloon, "the village blacksmith," of Meredith wrote a local history column for the *Meredith News* in the 1920s, and in it he remembered growing up in the 1850s and 1860s. According to U.S. Census records, Edgar Maloon was born in Meredith in 1852, the third son of Greenleaf and Polly Maloon. His father was a blacksmith, and Edgar followed in the trade. He married Augusta Graves of Sandwich, and they lived in Meredith Village next to Edgar's blacksmith shop. Edgar also owned a wheelbarrow manufacturing business, which he sold in 1909, and it became the long-running Prescott Lumber Company. Greenleaf Maloon's old stone blacksmith shop, where Edgar started work, was on Water Street and backed on the Waukewan Canal. Edgar wrote that "this was one of the very first shops in Meredith, owned and operated by David Corliss, who was an old man when I first knew him sixty or more years ago. The light came through holes in the wall which were closed by wooden shutters, there being no glass in the holes. In those old days the blacksmiths burned charcoal on their forge. This they had to buy when they could and store it in a house by itself."

He remembered that "in the rear of my father's shop was water from Measley Pond, now Lake Waukewan. There were plenty of shiners, a fish about four to six inches long. I used to catch these for Dr. Hosea Smith's hens, so many shiners for a stick of candy." Speaking of the site of the present three-story building across from today's post office at the corner of Main and High Streets, which was once the town hall, Maloon said:

> *Water stood where the town hall stands. Logs dropped into the water around Long Pond* [Lake Winona today], *and Measley Pond need not be removed*

> *until they reached here, when they were floated on to a low wheeled ox rig which was backed up into the water and the logs were floated onto the axle and chained. The team was then hitched on and the logs came to dry land. They were dragged down to the old up and down* [single vertical blade] *sawmill where John P. McKendrie made them into dimension lumber. We boys used to run over these logs. One day a brother of Mrs. John Roberts made a misstep and went down between the logs and was drowned.*[54]

Maud Weymouth grew up on her grandfather Daniel P. Smith's farm one mile outside Meredith Center village during the 1870s and 1880s. She remembered the mills, stores, blacksmith shops, the carpenter, the cobbler, the doctors, the keeper of the inn where the stagecoach stopped and ministers of the Freewill Baptist Church. One well-remembered business was the store kept for some sixty years by Lane Plummer. Meredith Center got its own post office in 1837, located in Lane Plummer's store, with Lane as the first postmaster. Maud wrote:

> *The writer remembers the man and recalls her experience not once but many times with him as postmaster. As a little girl she often "went for the mail." Sometimes an uncle, who was away, would send a postal regarding the time of his home-coming. Mr. Plummer would take the card from the box, adjust his spectacles with precision, read the card, then say: "Now you hurry right home, your Uncle Joe is coming on that 4 o'clock train, and wants your father to meet him." After his admonition I received the card with the added injunction not to lose it.*

Maud remembered Captain Bickford, who ran a store where "braided hats, butter, eggs and cheese [all made on the surrounding farms] were exchanged for West India molasses, rum and salt fish," and she remembered carpenter John Sanborn, who "was a wizard with tools."[55]

John Sanborn's son, Fred, born in 1845, also wrote his memories of growing up in Meredith Center. He worked for a time in the sawmill, which also produced shingles, noting, "I packed them in quarter-hundred bunches (enough to cover 25 square feet of roof) and received money for so doing. There was a knack or art even in doing this, good, wide, knotless shingles were put on the bottom and on top, which made them look well."

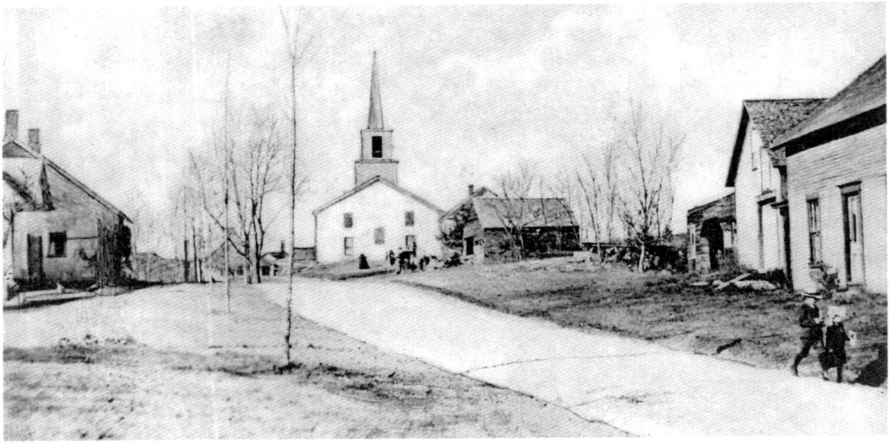

The steeple on Meredith Center's Freewill Baptist church was built by John Sanborn, who also raised the bell into place. *Meredith Historical Society.*

John Sanborn was responsible for planning and building the steeple on the Freewill Baptist Church. Fred recalled, "He drew the plan of the steeple and belfry, 'something to lift the meetinghouse up and make it look better,' that was his language. It did put style and finish to the church edifice. Other churches in this vicinity had no steeples and the Center church outshined [its] rivals which was gratifying to the parishioners."[56]

From 1754, when the Masonian proprietors extended Meredith's north boundary five miles to the east, where it met the boundary of Moultonborough, the village of Center Harbor was divided. Located at the head of Lake Winnipesaukee and at the intersection of roads to the east, west and north, the village grew to become an important transportation hub, with lodging, a church, a school, a post office and services, but it was only partly in the town of Center Harbor. The boundary line between the towns of Meredith and Center Harbor ran from west to east just north of the lakeshore, behind the present Congregational Church, fire department and town offices. The entire lakeshore was in the town of Meredith.

Center Harbor petitioned the legislature to grant it some Winnipesaukee lakeshore, and the request was granted in 1873, taking land from

Meredith, over its objections. Measured from the Moultonborough town line, the Meredith boundary was moved west some one and a half miles to where it is today. As a consolation, Meredith was entitled to continue to collect taxes from the residents and properties that it lost to Center Harbor for a period of five more years. The act went into effect on July 3, 1873, and the residents of Center Harbor celebrated a very merry Independence Day that year.

Chapter 13

MEREDITH'S EARLY BANDS

On Parade Road, south of where Pickerel Pond Road joins, the high flat fields were once the militia training ground. Militias made up of everyday male citizens were raised in time of war. After the War of 1812, the militia was made permanent, and this is where the military titles of many of our local historical figures came from. The local militia company—from Meredith, New Hampton, Sanbornton and Center Harbor—was known as the Winnipisiogee Guards. It trained, or "paraded," on this field, which gave Parade Road its name. Every male of military age was required by law to present himself, with his gun, knapsack, two flints and twenty cartridges, to participate in the drill. Families came along, too, as Carl Blaisdell noted:

> *These trainings, or musters as they were called, were gay and lively affairs. On training days crowds of people began arriving from all the surrounding country. The day assumed that of Old Home Day* [see chapter 18] *of our modern times. Women and children engaged in all sorts of entertainments. Vendors of all sorts of things came early on the scene, selling their wares, such as needles, pins and ribbons. The stores did a great business besides selling refreshments of all kinds, including gingerbread and old cider. Plenty of* [West] *Indian rum flowed freely, and by mid-morning its effects were quite noticeable on the training field.... Until the year 1845 these gatherings were held.*[57]

Music was needed for these military musters and for civic events, and local musicians formed a band for that purpose. The first Meredith band of record is the Moses Pease Band, probably composed of bugles and clarinets and led by Pease, who played the "keyed bugle." He was from the Pease Road area, and the band is remembered to have played for the musters held at the nearby Meredith Parade. It played "Over the Hills and Far Away," "Black Is the Color of My True Love's Hair," "Buffalo Gals," "The Old Oaken Bucket" and "Oh! Susannah," among others.

The three-valved "cornet" replaced the bugle after the Civil War. To be up-to-date, many bands began to call themselves "cornet bands" in the 1870s and 1880s, and this was when the Meredith Cornet Band got started. David Vittum of Meredith, who had earlier organized a boy's band, led the Meredith Cornet Band, with young George Sanborn—later founder of the *Meredith News* and Meredith Public Library—playing bass horn. Charles and John Pease, sons of Moses, played cornet in the Meredith band and later led Laconia's Belknap Cornet Band. Vittum also taught Center Harbor players, who became that town's long-lasting Cornet Band, led by Smith Emery. These bands played the old songs and new, popular ones like "Grandfather's Clock" and the Irish American "Sweet Rosie O'Grady" and "My Wild Irish Rose." Sheet music publishers did a brisk business issuing new hit songs. The temperance (prohibition) movement was gathering momentum at that time too. While their subject was deadly serious, they needed popular support and hired bands to play for their frequent rallies. David Vittum remembered that his band, although not officially for "temperance," was present to provide music at most of the meetings.[58]

The Meredith Cornet band dissolved, but in about 1885, David Vittum was approached to coach musicians for a new "Mechanics Band." They practiced in the "old band hall" above Beede's store at Plymouth and Main Streets. This band grew rapidly, and according to Vittum, "Its instrumentation was of such a nature that a different line of music was studied and performed than anything ever attempted by a Meredith band, and a reputation was established which reached over a large territory of the state."[59] Many people were moving from Meredith to Laconia, Manchester and other manufacturing centers at that time. Unfortunately, Vittum and other band members did so, too, and despite its renown, the Mechanics Band lasted but a few years.

Meredith had gotten used to having a good band, so when J.W. White moved to the village in 1893 to open a restaurant, it became known that he and Mrs. White were accomplished cornetists. They were asked to teach

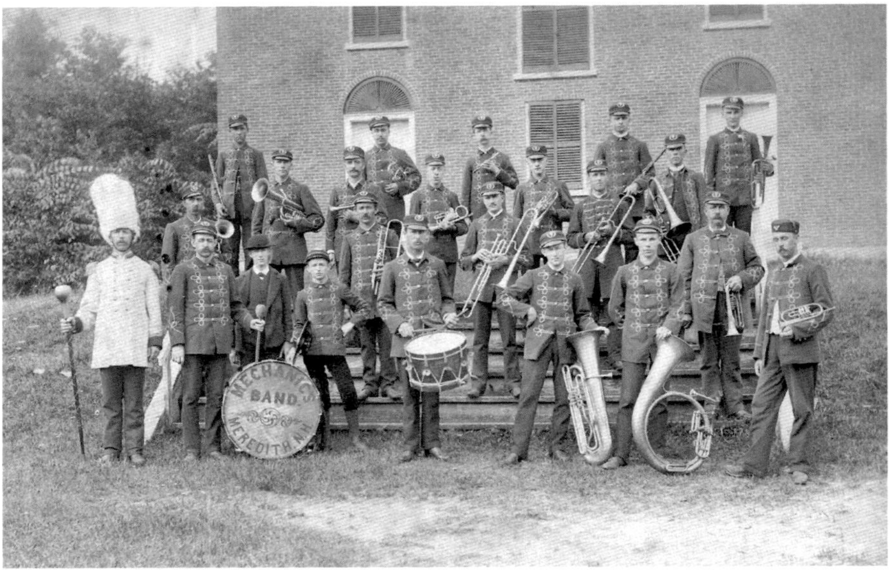

The Meredith Mechanics Band played for many events in the 1880s. *Meredith Historical Society.*

music and form a band. White's Silver Band was soon organized, outfitted in dark-red coats, dark-blue caps and white pants. They won first prize in a band competition at the Weirs in 1895, with Mrs. White as cornet soloist, and went on to perform as far away as Quebec.

The Whites moved from Meredith, and the band dissolved around 1900. Some members of that band and new recruits formed the Meredith Military Band in 1908. They appeared in uniform and were much in demand until the group ceased to practice or perform in early 1912. In about 1910, three young people—George Richardson, violin; Lillian Trombley, piano; and Carl Robinson, clarinet—formed what they called the Meredith Youth Orchestra and gained a wide reputation. Another Meredith band like the Silver and Military Bands was formed in 1921 and played until 1926. In 1930, Elsie Gerrish, a graduate of the New England Conservatory, organized twenty-two Meredith village schoolchildren aged seven to fourteen into the Meredith Junior Orchestra. They played for town events. School bands then became more commonplace than the private bands of old.

From its start in the militia muster period, there was a pattern in the history of bands. Many people played musical instruments at home or informally, and from David Vittum's descriptions of band organization, many people

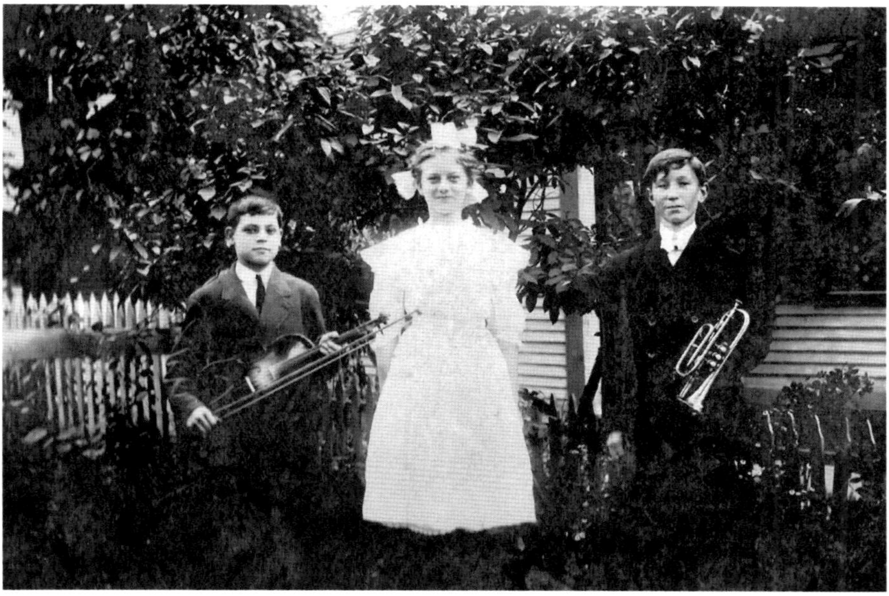

George Richardson, Lillian Trombley and Carl Robinson played together as the Meredith Youth Orchestra, circa 1910. *Meredith Historical Society.*

learned to play several instruments. What made a band was organization, leadership, recruitment and practice. A few people like the Peases, David Vittum and the Whites were interested enough and willing to undertake the work of organizing a band, worrying about the balance of instruments, learning about band music performance, recruiting members, providing instruction, getting uniforms, conducting practice, advertising and booking performances. The life of the band depended on the commitment of all the members, and other things often interceded. Members moved away, had family or business concerns or simply lost interest. A special case of longevity is the Center Harbor Band, which was organized in 1875 during the cornet band period and is still playing today.

Chapter 14

Sol Lovejoy and the Bear Island House

Due to its location, Meredith Neck was settled somewhat later than the territory between Meredith Bridge and Meredith Village. Among the early settlers in the southeast corner of the Neck shortly after 1810 were Caleb and Susannah Lovejoy and their four children. Their son Jesse stayed there to farm, and he and his wife, Eleanor, had two sons, Solomon and Ezra.

Solomon and Ezra were the third generation to live on the land settled by their grandfather, and the bond to their Meredith Neck neighborhood was strong. When Sol was born in 1844, the Lovejoy farm was being worked by his father, Jesse, and mother, Eleanor, while his father's brothers, David and Herbert, lived nearby. When he was twenty-nine, Sol married seventeen-year-old Sarah Elizabeth ("Lizzie") Wiggin, who grew up on a nearby Meredith Neck farm. The year after marrying Lizzie, Sol's first real estate transaction was to buy the forty-acre farm of George Bickford in 1875, bordering land of his uncles, David and Herbert Lovejoy. Here the newlyweds settled, in familiar surroundings, about halfway between Sol's and Lizzie's parents. Although Sol told the census taker in 1880 that he was a farmer, he was not remembered by his neighbors as being very active in that line of work. While he stayed in the family neighborhood, Sol found ways other than farming to earn a living from the land.

In the same 1875 land transaction, Sol also bought two acres near the active sawmill and shingle mill of Lucian Kelley on nearby Fish Brook. In 1877, he bought a five-acre parcel of adjoining land owned by James and

David Roberts, with a house in which David and Abbie Roberts were then living. The deed of sale allowed the Roberts to keep possession of their house and to move it off the lot if they so wished. Sol next acquired land on Lake Winnipesaukee in 1878, bordering his own land and that of his uncle Herbert. When his father, Jesse, died in 1880, Sol bought land adjoining the old meetinghouse cemetery and then sold burial plots there. That same year, Sol bought his brother Ezra's inherited share of the family land. In 1882, Sol went into the lumber milling business, buying a shingle mill on Fish Brook from the Robertses. He would later buy the Kelley sawmill and shingle mill, too—probably a longtime ambition.

Meanwhile, nearby Bear Island was becoming a popular destination for summer vacationers, who were staying at a boardinghouse owned by Waldo and Abigail Maloon and operated by Melissa and Leonard Davis. Sol, who had been born on Bear Island, saw his future as well as his past there and bought back fifty acres of his father's former island pastureland from the Maloons in 1882. In 1883, he purchased their boardinghouse, 120 surrounding acres and their three boats and went into the summer hotel business. Sol and Lizzie expanded the house into a forty-room hotel for up to one hundred guests; they hired staff and had vegetable gardens, chickens and milk cows enough to supply food for the hotel and the expanding summer cottage community on the island. The railroad steamers delivered guests to the hotel wharf from the Weirs and Alton Bay, and arriving passengers were met at the dock by the hotel's horse-drawn surrey. In 1886, Sol bought the Meredith Neck property where the Bear Island steamer landed, with storehouses, sheds and a workshop. When mail began to be delivered to the island in 1892, he became official postmaster of Bear Island's summer post office.

To enhance their Bear Island House hotel, the Lovejoys created clay tennis courts and a "lovers' lane" for carriage rides. The hotel commanded expansive views of Lake Winnipesaukee and the White and Ossipee Mountains over open fields. It had porches with rocking chairs from which guests could relax and take in the view. The property also offered "a delightful beach, with the finest sand and gradually deepening water," bathhouses, croquet and boats for hire. Guests could stroll the lanes of the island or take buggy rides, and the arrival of the steamers at the hotel dock was a popular diversion. The B&M steamer *Mt Washington* made three stops daily in 1902. From 1906, the steam mail boat *Uncle Sam* carried both mail and passengers twice daily. Hotel guests could tour the lake on these boats, and the Lovejoys' own boat was available for parties.

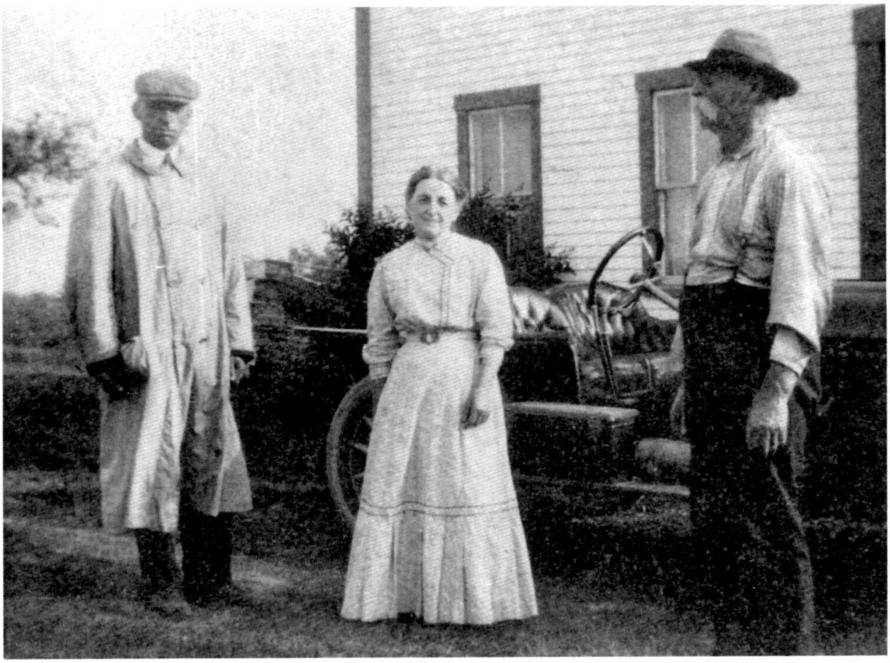

Ralph, Lizzie and Sol Lovejoy. *Meredith Historical Society.*

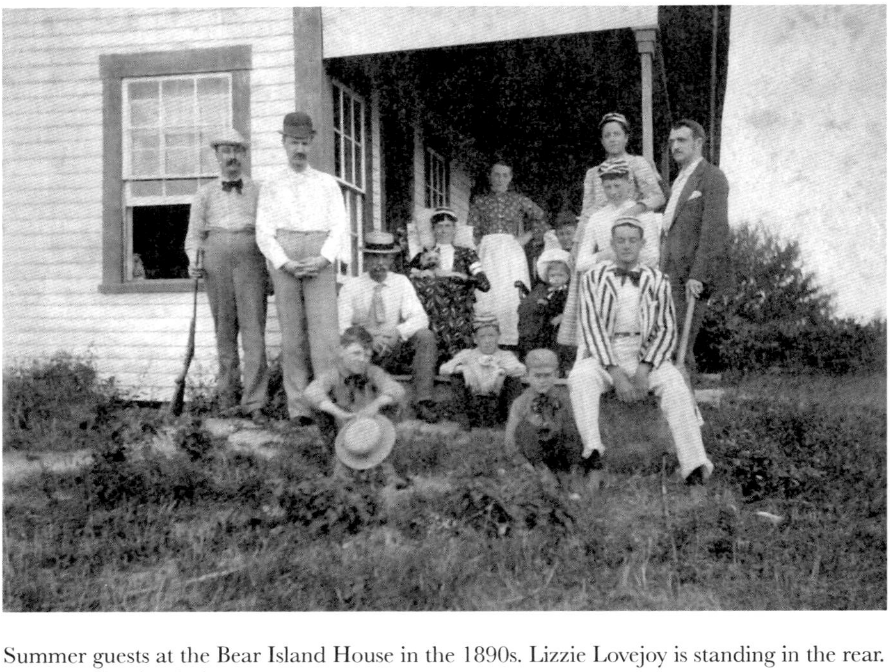

Summer guests at the Bear Island House in the 1890s. Lizzie Lovejoy is standing in the rear. *Meredith Historical Society.*

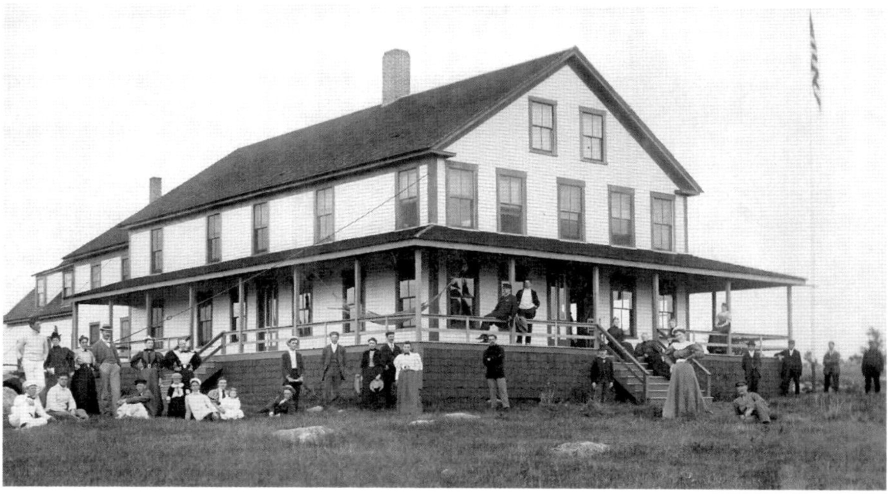

The Bear Island House before the Lovejoys added a second wing. *Meredith Historical Society.*

Guests usually spent two or more weeks, and many returned year after year. Easy familiarity with the place and the people was one of the charms of their summer vacation. Rates in 1902 were one dollar per day or five to seven dollars per week. The large staff boarded on site for the season, serving the guests and the island's summer residents who came to the dining room, making the hotel a bustling place for its employees.[60]

Sol subdivided his Bear Island land and sold many shorefront lots to eager cottagers, who also bought supplies from him, together with building lumber and shingles from his sawmills. During the winter, the hotel was closed, and the Lovejoys lived at their Meredith Neck house. Sol and Lizzie's son, Ralph, was born in 1884, growing up at their Meredith Neck home and spending summers at Bear Island. They sold the Bear Island House in 1909, with Sol holding the mortgage and continuing his active real estate business on the Neck. The registry of deeds recorded eighty-nine of Sol's transactions over his lifetime—the last a land sale to the (Shep) Browns in 1924, the year Sol died. Growing up at a time when the farming way of life was changing and people were moving away, Sol was nonetheless able to earn a living and stay in his ancestral neighborhood.

George Collins bought the Bear Island House from the Lovejoys and operated it until 1922, when it was purchased by Coleman Blair. Alice Rand Monty, who worked there as a waitress, remembered that "there was a menu for every meal and the food was very good…Some guests would take boat trips in a group so the hotel would put up lunches for them. Others just sat in the sunshine and rested…They had dances in the front room and the waitresses were allowed to mix with the guests. We enjoyed this as we met some very nice people."[61] The hotel brochure for 1915 mentioned that dances and "musicales" were frequent, but "we always insist upon the termination of all gaiety at a reasonable hour" in consideration of those who retire early.

Automobile tourism beginning in the 1920s led to the waning of the summer hotel era, along with the lessening of railroad and steamer service to tourist destinations. The depression of the 1930s dealt a further blow. At the end of the 1934 summer season, the empty hotel caught fire. Meredith firemen managed to save the barn and to remove much of the hotel furniture, including two pianos, but the Bear Island House was not rebuilt. Today, just the foundation remains. The Town of Meredith took over the former hotel dock, where the mail continues to be delivered today for Bear Island summer residents.

Chapter 15

From Livery Stable to Library

The first libraries in New Hampshire were private or "social" libraries, chartered by the legislature as corporations, with officers and all the business powers that corporations have. They benefited only their members, who paid subscriptions to have access to the books. Even as land was being cleared and roads were being cut in the new towns of the Lakes Region, libraries were being founded. Tamworth had a social library in 1796, followed by Sanbornton in 1797, a joint Moultonborough-Sandwich corporation in 1800, Meredith Bridge (later to become Laconia) in 1807 and Center Harbor in 1829. The scientific/technological revolution was well underway in Europe by the 1790s, and Americans did not want to be left behind. People in the then remote new towns of the Lakes Region were building farms, mills and businesses and did not want to be out of touch. In the nineteenth century, the popular belief was that knowledge led to progress, and progress led to prosperity. Social libraries were the result of a need for information that had already outstripped most individuals' ability to buy books and periodicals for themselves.

Meanwhile, progressive political forces were at work in the United Kingdom and the United States—led in this country by New Hampshire. The New Hampshire legislature passed an act in 1849 allowing towns to use taxes to establish public libraries, a year before the U.K. parliament passed its own similar measure. By this law, towns could raise and appropriate money to buy land; erect library buildings; buy books, maps, charts and periodicals; and pay staff. As progressive as public libraries might have been, New Hampshire towns were losing population and tax income in the late 1800s, and it would take something more to establish public libraries. In many towns, individuals stepped forward; in Meredith, it was George Sanborn.

George F. Sanborn, the son of Meredith's venerable Dr. George Sanborn, was a restless innovator. At the age of eighteen in 1875, he was well established enough as a printer to tackle the printing of the annual town report. He did this and other printing jobs in the Sanborn family home next to the current historical society. In 1880, he began a newspaper, the *Meredith Weekly News*, later to become the *Meredith News*, and in 1882, he decided to establish a public library. Meredith Village at that time was dominated by the Hodgson Hosiery Mill, the Shook and Lumber Mill, the George H. Clark Lumber Company, many boardinghouses for the millworkers, blacksmith shops, livery stables and a string of businesses along Main Street.

Sanborn's newspaper and library initiatives were attempts to improve the cultural resources of the community. He began a subscription drive to raise money to buy and transport a collection of eight hundred books made available by former Meredith resident John Smith Jr. of Boston. The public response to Sanborn's campaign was positive and prompt. He bought the books, built bookshelves in a room in the Sanborn home, printed a catalogue of the titles and assumed the job of librarian. The 1882 Meredith town meeting voted $100 to cover Sanborn's expenses for "care of books, coal and light," and a board of trustees was formed. The new Meredith Public Library began life at the top of a flight of stairs on the second floor of the Sanborn home, along with space devoted to the *Meredith News* office.

Others later served as librarians, and the library grew and moved several times to other buildings in the village. The threat of fire was constant in Meredith at that time, so when former resident Benjamin M. Smith offered in 1899 to donate a brick and granite library building in memory of his parents, there was considerable interest. Smith, who was also community-minded, wanted the town to purchase and clear a derelict property next to the Baptist church as a condition of his donation. That lot contained the neglected Collins boardinghouse, but perhaps more importantly, its barn housed Edwin Cox's livery stable, and Cox was a selectman.[62]

Livery stables were at the heart of every town. Farmers coming to town to conduct business needed to have their horses watered and fed. Those who lived in town but lacked a barn needed to have their horses boarded and perhaps have their buggy or sleigh stored. People visiting the town by train needed a horse or horse and buggy to get out into the countryside,

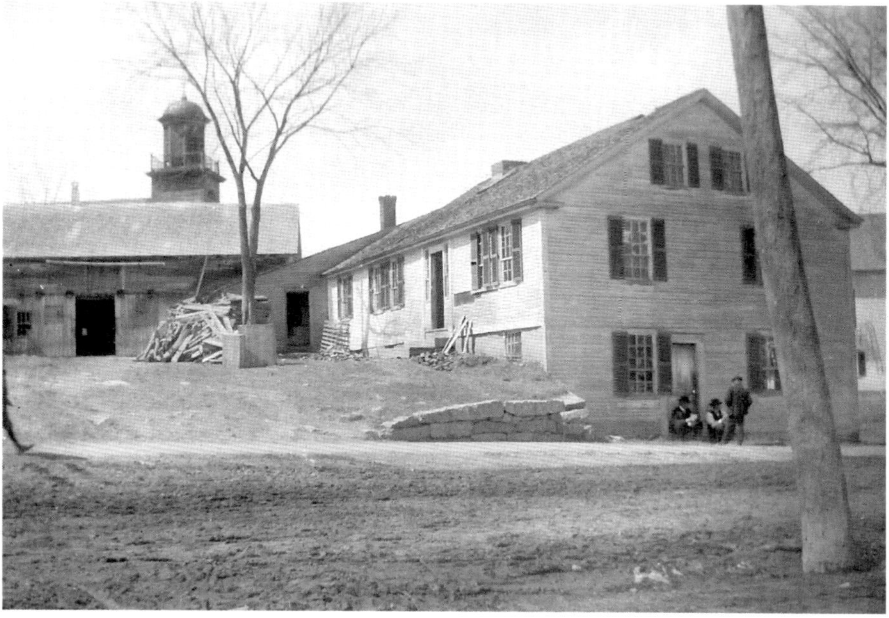

The Collins boardinghouse and its barn, which housed Edwin Cox's livery stable, became the site of today's Meredith Public Library. *Meredith Historical Society.*

and those traveling by horse and buggy needed overnight accommodation for their horse as well as themselves. Around 1900, the going rate for day-boarding a horse was twenty-five cents, and the rate for water, oats, hay and a stall overnight was one dollar. Livery stables, whether independently run or owned by hotels, did a lively business. Sundays and holidays were busy, as those were the days that people, including courting couples, took buggy rides for pleasure. The larger livery stables offered a variety of vehicles too: victorias, coupes, surreys, phaetons, buckboards and buggies. Name signs advertising livery stables usually featured a horse's head, and print advertisements followed suit. The liveryman usually bought new horses in the spring to be ready for the summer trade and sold some off in the fall, when business dropped off. People tended to be less careful with livery horses and equipment or even abuse them, so the liveryman needed to repair vehicles, harnesses and saddles and to be a doctor for his horses. Livery horses were sometimes used for one-way trips, in which case arrangements with other cooperating stables had to be maintained; sometimes miscreants simply abandoned livery horses. College students had an especially bad reputation with liverymen.

As useful as the livery stable was to the community, its reputation was not always the best. The stable could usually be located by the smell. Edwin Mitchell noted that, "Of all the odors of the horse and buggy age none was so powerful or abiding as that of the livery stable. They all had an atmosphere that was redolent of damp straw, ammonia, and manure." Living near a stable also was unattractive for the daily and nightly noise of iron-shod horses tramping over the wooden flooring, stamping and kicking the sides of their stalls. Mitchell went on to note that flies "swarmed about a livery stable like bees around a honey pot" and that "rats, too, were very bad." The human element at the stable might also be cause for concern. Stablemen tended to be rough-edged, and those residents of the town with nothing else to do often congregated at the stable. Popular but illegal dogfights and cockfights were often held behind the closed doors of livery stables.[63]

In Meredith village, Edwin Cox's livery stable—with eight horses and twenty carriages for hire early in the year 1900—was next to the Baptist church in a barn behind and attached to the Collins boardinghouse. Smith's offer to put a new library on this lot, if the town would buy and clear it, was an issue on the warrant for the 1900 town meeting. Cox was a selectman up for reelection and opposed acceptance of Smith's offer. However, the vote was 201 in favor of acceptance and only 1 opposed. Also in that election, George F. Sanborn was elected selectman, defeating incumbent Cox. The town bought the property, and Smith began building the library, which was designed by the architectural firm of Charles Hawkins and George Swan. Benjamin Smith then came often from Massachusetts to Meredith to oversee the construction of the handsome brick and granite library, with its slate roof, molded copper gutters and ridge trim, "town clock" in the front gable and ash-paneled interior with fireplaces. The building featured electric lighting, plumbing, central heat and a fireproof vault for storage of the town records. Edwin Cox was able to keep the buildings of his livery stable, but he had to move them to another location.

Looking into Benjamin Smith's family history, historian Rudy VanVeghten uncovered a skeleton—Benjamin's older brother, John—whose 1860s service as Meredith selectman was investigated for financial irregularities and who left town following personal bankruptcy. This was the same John Smith Jr. who supplied the library's first books in 1882, and it may be that both John's and Benjamin's library efforts were intended to restore the family's good name in Meredith.

Meanwhile, civic leader and Civil War veteran Major Edwin Bedee donated a statue to the property commemorating the service of the Twelfth

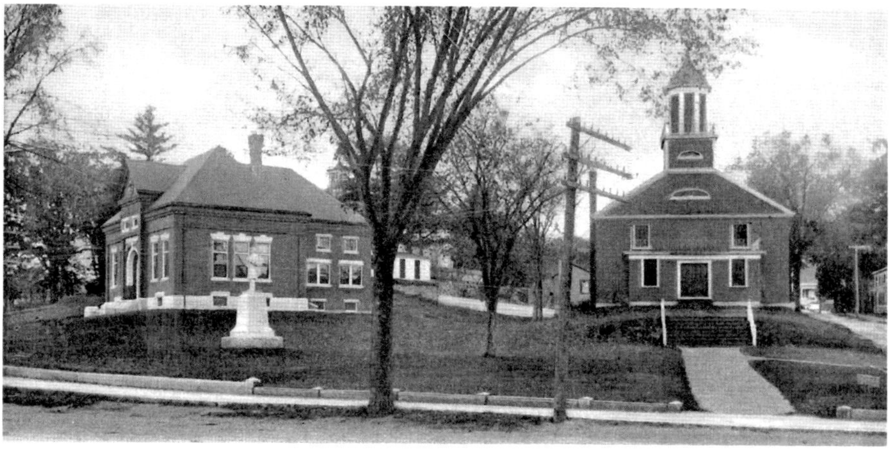

The new brick Meredith Public Library, the memorial to the Twelfth New Hampshire Regiment and the Baptist church. *Meredith Public Library.*

New Hampshire Regiment. Bedee had served with distinction, was the first person to assist fatally wounded President Lincoln at Ford's Theater and later became wealthy mining diamonds in Africa.

The new library building was dedicated on June 17, 1901. Selectman Fred Smith offered these words on behalf of the town: "Resolved, that we pledge ourselves properly to use and care for the gift and gratefully to remember the giver in future years." Benjamin Smith then ceremonially handed the keys to the building to Selectman George F. Sanborn, founder of the Meredith Public Library in 1882.

Chapter 16

Rural Free Delivery on Land and Water

As new methods of transportation came into use, the Post Office Department began contracting them to carry the mail. First there were horseback post riders, and then came stagecoaches. In 1823, Congress declared waterways to be post roads so steamboats could carry the mail, and in 1838, railroads began to do so. Where steamboats and trains did not go, stagecoaches continued to carry mail, even into the twentieth century, as from the Meredith railroad station to Center Harbor, Moultonborough and Sandwich.

Before the 1890s, rural people had to go to the post office for their mail. There were many post offices of different classifications around the countryside to make that somewhat easier, but it was still an inconvenience compared with the home mail delivery that people in towns enjoyed. The Post Office Department experimented with Rural Free Delivery (RFD) during the 1890s and made it standard nationwide in 1902. By that time, there were already 8,500 RFD mail carriers. The project required not just trained mailmen but also good roads and standardized mailboxes. People could buy mass-produced metal boxes stamped "Approved by the Postmaster General" or make their own weatherproof versions. The RFD carrier had to pass a civil service exam and furnish his own transportation. In the early years, a horse and wagon were standard, but by 1929, the Post Office Department reported that most carriers had automobiles.[64]

The *Meredith News* reported on one carrier's typical summer day during the late 1920s. It began at 6:20 a.m., when the carrier arrived at the post office to "case" the letters, packages, COD parcels and catalogues for the boxes to which he had to deliver them along his route—starting with the first RFD mailbox and ending with the last. Then the morning "paper train" pulled into the station and unloaded the day's first-class mail and up to forty mailbags of newspapers, packages and magazines. This, too, had to be cased according to each rural box to which it should be delivered. Then he needed to load his car, fill it with gas on the way out and deliver mail to the boxes on both sides of the road as he followed his route. Along the way were "extension routes," such as Camp Kuwiyan, full of children who were sending and receiving huge quantities of mail, or the training camp of professional boxer Jack Delaney, who was getting ready for his next fight. Many summer cottages had been opened, so the volume of mail to be delivered along the lakeshore was substantial. His route included some 125 boxes, and on that Wednesday, he finished by early afternoon.

The RFD mailman did not just handle letters, newspapers and magazines. He also handled parcel post and money orders, collected for COD mail, managed Registered Mail and sold stamps and postcards. The 1920s were the heyday of Sears-Roebuck and other catalogues and mail-order shopping, so the volume of mail was large. The mailman's car was a traveling post office, and his job varied with the season. Even as late as the 1920s, rural roads were not plowed in the winter. The snow was packed down by a heavy, horse-drawn roller, so RFD carriers switched to horse-drawn sleighs. Rural roads were not paved, so during the spring mud season, the carrier needed to resort again to a horse and wagon. The RFD mailman was probably the only federal employee most people ever met, and he was a source of advice and a carrier of news. He did favors for his customers, who were also his friends, except for giving rides in the mail vehicle, which was strictly forbidden by the Post Office Department.[65]

One RFD carrier's daughter remembered that her father always had interesting news and stories to share at the supper table. For a time, he traded in his car and bought a new one every year. She recalled that "one of my happiest memories goes back to the nights when I walked with my father along the street carrying a lantern to a small barn where he kept the horse he used in winter. I loved helping him feed the horse his hay and grain and making sure he had plenty of water."[66]

In addition to RFD, the Post Office Department had earlier created Railway Post Offices (RPOs). When trains began carrying the mail in 1838, they simply carried it between post offices, but in 1864, the Railway Post Office was created. In this new system, a rail car became a post office and processed the mail en route. Later, this concept was extended to boats and

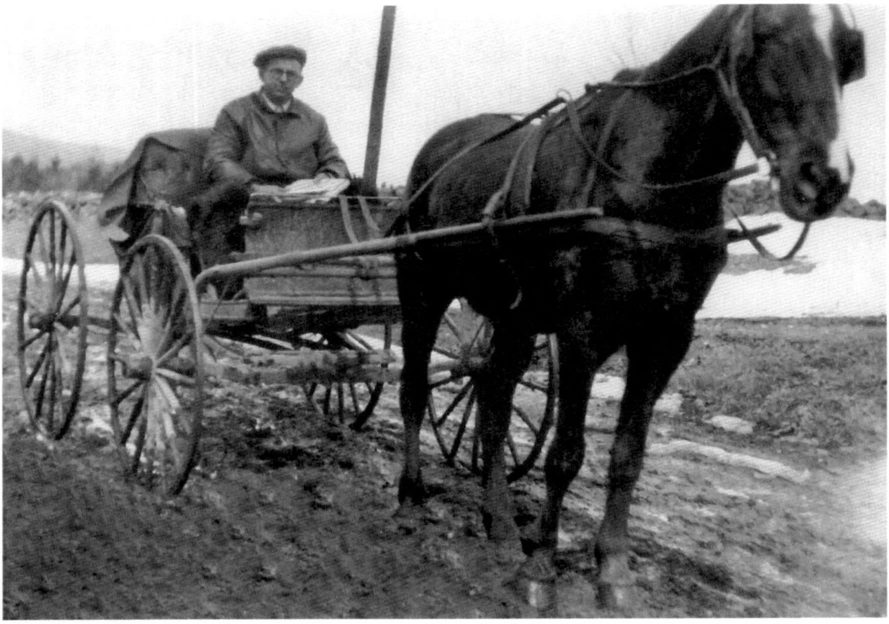

RFD carrier Ray Pickering delivering the mail in mud season. *Meredith Historical Society.*

came to be used on Winnipesaukee and Squam Lakes. While the department was still experimenting with the concept of Rural Free Delivery, RFD Route no. 7 was established in 1892 to deliver mail around Lake Winnipesaukee by boat from the Lakeport Post Office. The first mail boat was the steamer *Robert & Arthur*, followed by the *Dolphin* in 1894. Then in 1906, the *Uncle Sam* came into service. This was a large steamer, sixty-five feet long by fourteen feet in beam and capable of carrying one hundred passengers.

Along with delivering and picking up mail at many islands that had summer residents or children's camps, these boats carried passengers who enjoyed the ride and the scenery. By 1914, the *Uncle Sam* had become an RPO, providing post office services and processing mail en route. Other RPO boats served the eastern side of the lake, based in Wolfeboro and Alton Bay. Letters mailed from one location on the lake received the RPO cancellation and could be delivered to another lakeside location on the same day. The RPO boat also handled registered and certified letters, stamp sales, parcel post, money orders and other standard post office services. In 1903, the steamer *Halcyon* began delivering mail around Squam Lake, and it, too, became an RPO. The last year of Squam Lake mail service was 1969.

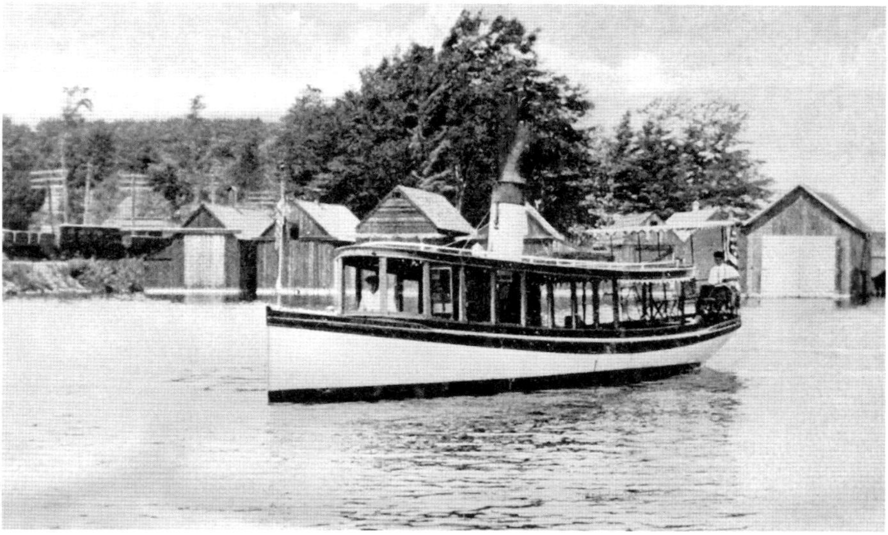

The steamer *Dolphin* delivered mail and carried passengers from Lakeport to several Lake Winnipesaukee islands. *Meredith Historical Society.*

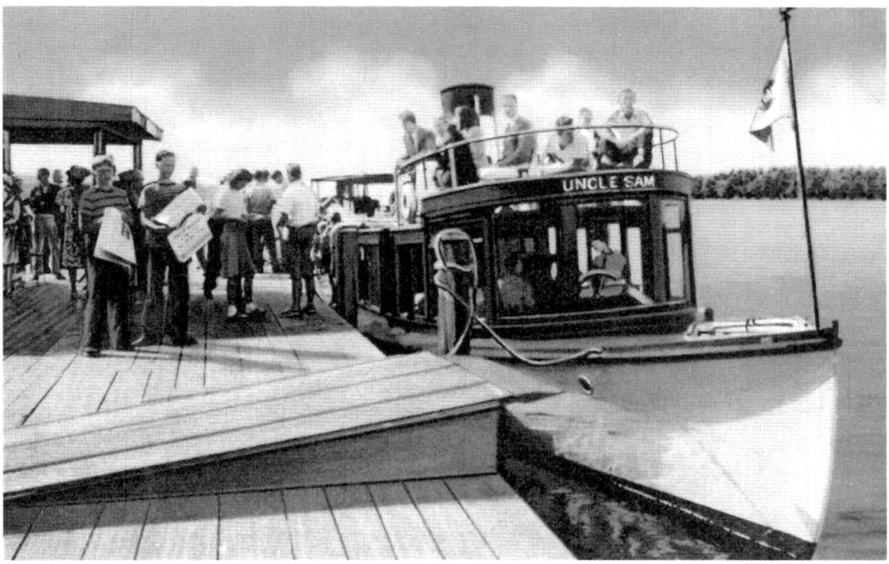

The mail boat *Uncle Sam* delivering mail to the Bear Island dock in the 1940s. *Meredith Historical Society.*

While not an RPO, airmail delivery was provided on Lake Winnipesaukee by Bob Fogg's flying service during the summer of 1925. The Post Office Department began awarding contracts to flying companies to carry the mail, and Fogg was contracted to provide airmail delivery in his open cockpit Curtiss flying boat. Operating from his Weirs seaplane base and picking up the incoming mail from the 5:55 a.m. train, he flew fifty miles daily around the lake, making ten stops. He was back at the Weirs in time to put the outgoing mail on the 8:05 a.m. train to Boston. Fogg flew alone, carried the mail in the passenger seats, landed offshore and taxied in at each stop. There a mail clerk met him and had to help him turn around—standing in the water. Fogg could not fly in bad weather, so he taxied his plane around the entire fifty-mile route.[67] That experiment was not repeated, but the mail boats *Uncle Sam* and *Uncle Sam II*—captained by Edward Lavalle—continued to provide RPO mail service on Lake Winnipesaukee for many years. Today, it is the *Sophie C.* that continues the floating post office tradition, carrying passengers and processing mail from the Weirs to Loon, Bear, Three Mile, Birch, Sandy, Cow and Jolly Islands.

Chapter 17

Farm Life in the 1920s

The strategy of Meredith farmers for many years had been "mixed farming." There were few places in town where large fields of cash crops could be planted, so farm families raised stock; planted some potatoes, corn or grain; grew fruits and vegetables for the market; produced milk, butter and cheese; made maple syrup and sugar; practiced various crafts; or worked part time at a trade. Some farmers went to work in logging camps during the winter. By the 1920s, the vacation boardinghouse era was coming to an end, but committed farm families could still make a living and enjoy it by doing a variety of things on their land. Work and play were governed by the seasons.

At the end of winter, damage to stone walls and fences by ice and fallen trees had to be repaired before the animals could be turned out to pasture, and fields had to be protected before they could be planted. Keeping sheep usually meant adding posts and wire to the tops of stone walls. The farmer carried posts at least six feet long to be driven vertically down into the wall, an iron bar to make the opening between the stones and an axe or hammer to drive the posts securely into place. He also carried wire and staples to make the wall-top fence.[68] If there were trees along the edge of the pasture, wire could be stapled to them. The growing tree soon absorbed this wire, which can be found today sticking out of the middle of trees along a boundary—the bane of surveyors and other modern boundary walkers.

Oxen or horses drew the plows to break the ground, but that resulted in large chunks of sod that had to be broken further. A "harrow" (a wheeled frame with teeth that could be pulled over the field to break up the clumps) was used for this purpose, but it needed to make several passes from different directions. New rocks worked their way into the plow zone each winter and had to be picked up and carried to piles inside the field or to the stone walls surrounding it. Today, stone walls can be identified as field or pasture walls by the size of the rocks they contain: pasture walls have uniformly large rocks, while walls that enclosed fields have rocks of varying sizes.

Once the ground was prepared, furrows were opened to receive seed. New England farmers became experts at detouring their rows around boulders and rock piles while keeping the whole pattern relatively parallel. The main row crops were corn, beans and potatoes. When the plants began to grow, the field needed to be cultivated and hoed by hand to remove weeds. A good farmer hoed his fields twice before the Fourth of July. Crows threatened the young corn plants, pulling them from the ground shortly after they sprouted. Some farmers looked for and raided crows' nests to capture the young birds, which they raised as pets. The belief was that having a crow in the yard would scare others from the surrounding fields.[69]

Farmers' grazing animals were European imports, and so was the "English hay" that they grew. Native grasses did not stand up to grazing by imported animals, so the early settlers had sown ryegrass, timothy, alfalfa, clover and other European forage plants, which made up Meredith hayfields from then on. Hayfields, or "mowing" fields, usually produced two crops in a growing season. The farmer watched the growth and ideally was able to cut his hay during a two-week window when the plants' leaves were full and the seed was just short of maturity. The first mowing was usually in June and the second in August or September. In rural Meredith in the 1920s, horse-drawn mechanical mowers were being used, as they had been since the late 1800s. Once cut, the grass needed to be "shook-out" with a pitchfork and spread to dry—a task often done by children. Then a horse-drawn hay rake was used to make windrows (long piles). When the piled hay had dried, a wheeled "hay rack" was pulled into the field by horses or oxen, and the hay was pitched up into it with pitchforks. There needed to be a pattern to this, so that the same bundles of hay that had been pitched into the rack could be pitched out again into the barn—work for men and teenagers. The whole operation was weather-dependent, often requiring postponements for the hay to re-dry or a mad rush to the barn to beat an oncoming rainstorm. If wet or green hay were placed in the barn, spontaneous combustion could easily start a devastating fire. If done properly, a year's feed and a special fragrance filled the farmer's barn.[70]

Farm girl Esther Carleton Wyatt remembered that "picking of all kinds of berries was a large occupation in our lives," from the few red and spicy-tasting "checkerberries" that they found in the woods in early spring to strawberries in June for shortcake, in biscuits or in bowls of cream, wild raspberries in July and, finally, blueberries. They picked high bush blueberries in their pasture, "around the end of haying so we had more time to concentrate on them. This was a real cash crop for us too, one for which we girls also received money.... We received twenty to twenty-five cents per quart early in the season but only fifteen cents in the later part." Esther wrote in her diary that they picked 296 quarts of berries one year, probably not counting those used in pies and biscuits and for canning. Farm families did not count their labor as an expense, but Esther's recollections show how important it was.[71]

Fall was a time for harvesting corn, potatoes and grain—some for market, but a good portion for storage in the barn as winter feed for cows, oxen, horses, pigs, chickens and sheep. It was a time for making cider and for storing apples, pumpkins, cabbages and root crops in the cellar, where home-canned goods, butter and cheese were also kept. A special process was used to make and store applesauce. First, fresh cider was boiled down to a syrup. Then, peeled and cored apples, with perhaps some quinces for flavor, were cooked in the syrup. The finished applesauce was stored in barrels or jars in the cellar. In the 1920s, most rural Meredith farms did not have electricity or even ice for refrigeration, so the cellar was used for storage—remaining cold, but above freezing through the winter. Dried herbs, spices, peas and beans were stored in the attic.

Esther recalled passing the 1920s winters in her family's un-insulated house, without central heat or electricity. A few rooms were heated by woodstoves, for which her father cut all the wood. Although the house and barn were connected by sheds, she remembered that "it was still very cold and we always dressed as if going outdoors." Esther carried a lantern for her father through the sheds to the barn to milk the cows in the winter's dark early mornings and evenings. The animals—cows, horses, oxen, sheep and chickens—had to be fed daily from the hay and feed stored in the barn. Esther's father needed to have at least half his corn and half his hay still on hand by Groundhog Day (February 2) in order to carry his animals through the winter. The animals were let out each day to go to a spring that was kept open for water so that Esther, her sisters and father could clean out the animals' stalls. They shoveled the manure down into the barn basement, where it was kept to spread on the fields in spring.[72]

The family's water was drawn daily by bucket from an outside well and heated on the kitchen stove, while wood for the kitchen and parlor stoves was brought in from the shed. Meat from animals butchered in the fall was kept frozen in a cold, unused front bedroom, and Esther's mother would bring pieces to the kitchen to thaw. That cold room also held tubs of lard—made at home from the fat of the stored pork—and bags of flour and sugar. After the animals were cared for, the corn husked and the cornstalks shredded for feed, the dried beans picked over for sale to the store and time taken to attend the local one-room school, Esther remembered having fun.

Her mother and father read aloud, and each family member read books borrowed from the library, which was six miles away and reached by horse and sleigh. There were parlor games like Parcheesi, dominoes and checkers; card games; and indoor hide-and-seek and blind man's bluff. They hunted for their Christmas tree in the nearby woods and pastures and trimmed it for the holiday. Esther remembered doing a good deal of sledding, called "sliding," on some long local hills or on the snow-covered roads—there being no cars out in the winter. They used barrel staves—two and a half feet long—as skis until Esther's father hand-sawed and planed real skis from straight ash logs. Girls were not supposed to wear pants, so Esther and her sisters skied in dresses, with bloomers and petticoats underneath and long underwear on their legs, covered by dark stockings. Much of their clothing, coats and mittens were made by their mother, who also hand-washed their clothes, hanging them "in the attic over the kitchen, where they would dry in a few days." Almost all of this winter activity took place on their farm or within walking distance—a small winter world.[73]

Rural roads were just beginning to be plowed in the late 1920s, and Esther's was not one of them. She wrote, "During the winter then, the roads were kept open by various farmers, using a short bobsled with blocks attached to the runners [and] drawn by horses, or in my father's place by oxen. The sleighs or sleds we used with the horse had the shafts offset to one side so the horse could walk on the broken track to pull the sleigh." Thus, the roads were passable when snow-covered and as long as the ground was frozen. With the warming of the ground, wagons replaced sleighs, but "sometimes with a trickle of water underneath, the top crust would suddenly give way and the horse or wagon would break through, often causing a broken shaft, or wheel, or...hurt the horse as he tried to move on in the muddy place.... Going to school, my folks drove us in the morning with the horse and buggy when the road was frozen, but by the afternoon it had thawed, and we walked home."[74]

When Esther went to high school in 1928, even the road between Meredith Center and Meredith Village was unpaved. "In the spring the road was just a solid mass of ruts with just no place for a horse to walk. So at that time, my sisters and I stayed over in the village during the week. On Friday afternoons, we walked as far as Meredith Center, where my father or mother would meet us with the horse and buggy to give us a ride home." Regarding mud season, she wrote:

> *As soon as possible, my father started scraping the roads with his oxen, dragging a wooden scraper to fill in the ruts and help the road dry faster. He did keep track of his hours very conscientiously, and sent a bill to the town and was paid at the rate of 50 cents an hour for himself and his oxen. About the last of May, the town road machine went over all the town roads, drawn earlier by horses, later by tractor. Several employees followed to pick rocks and clean culverts. Culverts now made of metal were then made by laying two lines of rocks and then covering them with large, flat rocks for what was then called a stone "cassy".... After the big machine and the men finished and left, we felt we had a wonderful road and mud season was over until next year.*[75]

There were few gasoline vehicles used on Meredith family farms in the 1920s, simply because the planted fields were too small for it to be practical

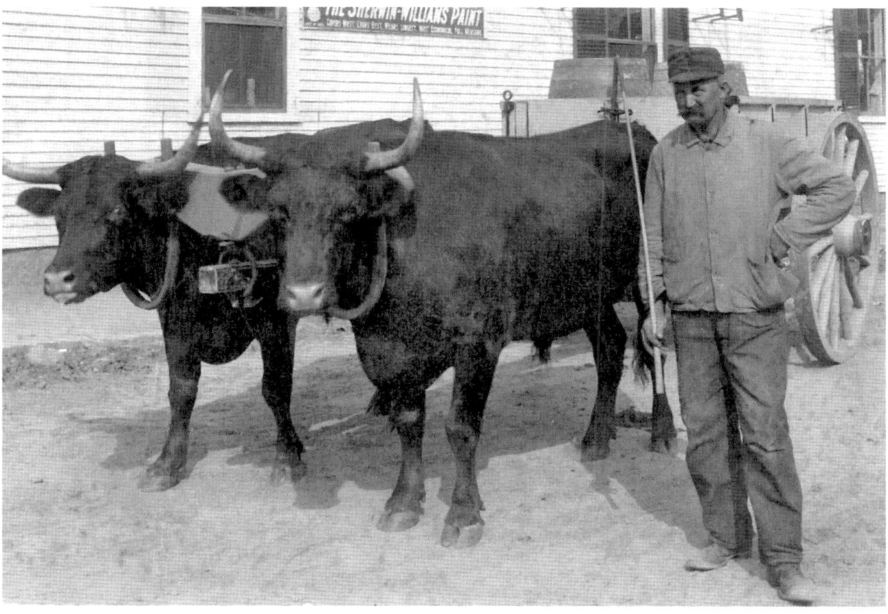

Meredith farmers continued using animal power into the 1930s. *Meredith Historical Society.*

or economical. Farmers continued to use horse-drawn haying equipment because they already had it, and the job was too time-sensitive to hire it done by machines. Cars, mostly Ford Model Ts, began to be used for travel but were put away in the barn during the winter. Non-mechanized family farms were still labor-intensive, and as families became smaller, so did the output of the farms.

Chapter 18

Farms for Summer Homes and Old Home Week

From the 1860s to the early twentieth century, people left New Hampshire farms to move west or work in the mill centers. Lacking enough young labor to keep on, many older farmers scaled back and had trouble paying their taxes. When they died, the farms often were abandoned. In about the year 1916, Fred Sanborn wrote:

> *When I was a boy, Meredith Center was something of a place. I remember when there were two stores, a woolen mill, wool carding mill, grist mill, saw mill. They have all gone except the latter, and that is silent most of the time.... Sixteen reasonably good farms have dropped out since I left school here* [about 1875]. *These are within a mile and a half radius of where I'm writing.... These farms have been abandoned and are growing up to wood and timber, principally pine.*

Meredith Center's mills had been small. The decline of sheep-raising and of farming in general beginning in the 1850s was a triple blow—cutting local sources of raw material for the mills, cutting the demand for services (blacksmiths, wheelwrights, shoemakers, carpenters, storekeepers and others who served farmers) and cutting population. Many service villages like Meredith Center lost their farm-related businesses during this time. Towns and the state lost tax revenue.

The Meredith tax records for 1890 to 1910 show that liens placed on properties due to taxes owed to the town grew steadily. Investors would bid on the property liens, paying the tax and incidental charges and obtaining the lien. In 1909, a lien on "200 feet shore Lake Winnisquam" was sold for unpaid taxes of $3.50, and a lien on a "farm cottage and land on shore Lake Winnipesaukee and ½ frame Lovejoy place" sold at tax auction for $2.80. The tax collector's records show that just one or two investors bought liens on whole lists of farms, houses, woodlots, pastures, island properties and commercial real estate at these auctions. One such buyer in 1910 paid $33.71 for liens on the houses and farms of twelve Meredith residents. If the tax went unpaid by the property owner for five years, the investor owned the property. In 1911, an investor holding a lien obtained ownership of thirty acres of land and buildings for $5.61, and in 1912, another obtained the "Eaton Farm," valued at $3,000, for $60.15.

Nahum Batchelder, secretary of the New Hampshire Board of Agriculture, attacked this problem in 1890 with a booklet, *Secure a Home in New Hampshire, Where Comfort, Health and Prosperity Abound*. Later titled *New Hampshire Farms for Summer Homes*, it was issued annually until 1915. As the titles suggest, the effort was aimed at attracting purchasers for abandoned or for-sale farms as vacation homes, and it was successful. Between 1890 and 1905, sixty-one Meredith farms were bought as summer homes. In 1904, there were twenty-five Meredith farms hosting summer visitors, and money spent for entertainment in town by summer visitors was reported at $60,000.[76]

The tax loss and farm abandonment problem also bothered Governor Frank W. Rollins, who cannily created "Old Home Week" as an event in 1899. He announced, "I have a scheme which I think promises to help the state, and which I hope to see put into execution. It is this, to have a week in summer set apart to be called Old Home Week, and to make it an annual affair."[77] The strategy was to invite former residents to return to their old towns for festivities, reunions with family and old friends and visits to fondly remembered homes, villages and landscapes.

Rollins asked the board of agriculture to promote the event and to assist towns in organizing it. Towns needed to compile address lists of former residents in order to send the invitations. They needed to organize parades, athletic events, church services, concerts, orations, fireworks and picnics. For an attention-getting kickoff on Saturday, August 26, 1899, the state coordinated the lighting of bonfires on mountain and hilltops "from Coos to the sea." Through this annual event, Rollins wanted to rekindle the returnees' attachment to the land, to prompt them to buy abandoned farms for second homes and to showcase the state's scenic and recreational resources. Soon the board of agriculture was receiving reports from participating towns that the scheme was working: real estate sales picked up, and donations for historic preservation, conservation and civic improvements were received. "By 1904, the board was able to report that some one hundred towns were holding either an Old Home Week or an Old Home Day each year, "strengthening the attachment to the old farm home among thousands of absent sons and daughters."[78]

Meredith was one of the towns that made Old Home Day an annual event, and the *Meredith News*' headline of August 25, 1926, read, "Old Home Day Exercises Were the Very Best Ever." The *News*' report of the event gave a particularly vivid picture: "Nearly every business place from the railroad station [today's lumberyard] to the old oak tree [today's Scenic Park], and many residences were beautifully decorated with bunting and flags, and banners, pennants and flags were hung across Main Street." Special mention went to Sanborn's Drug Store, Meredith Village Savings Bank, Pynn's Garage and residence, Piper Meat Market, the Elm Hotel and the Electric Light building, but all the stores, the post office and the *News* office were decorated.

A street parade in the morning was led by mounted girls and boys from summer camps and included a band and floats. The afternoon began with a band concert on the Baptist church lawn and then moved to town hall for a piano duet, an original poem of welcome, an address by the mayor of

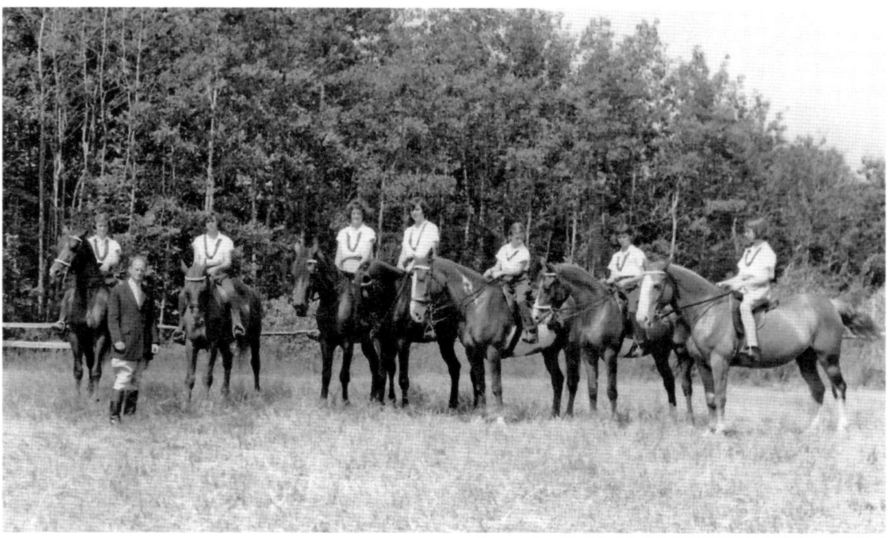

Camp Kuwiyan girls were among the summer campers who rode horses in Meredith's Old Home Day parade. *Meredith Historical Society.*

Nashua, a local speaker on New Hampshire's scenic beauty and prospects and a vocal solo, "The Big Brown Bear," with piano accompaniment. An original essay about a returning native was read, describing how "[t]o this woman, no longer young, the air of her native town is like wine. Our traveler gazes long across the shimmering blue waters of the old lake. Truly, she thinks, on the shore of this lake angels might find a resting place when bearing blessings, they descend to earth. She softly repeats the words: Oh, the years may bring their changes/And afar our steps may roam/But forever in our hearts/Will dwell our dear old home."[79] Three more addresses led to the singing of "America" by the audience to close the program.

Chapter 19

MEREDITH FOR CHILDREN

Camps Kuwiyan, Waldron and Andover

Lake Winnipesaukee offered a very rustic shoreline setting in the 1800s. Development was confined to the lakeside villages and to the few locations where resort hotels such as the Hotel Weirs, the Lakeside House and the Hotel Winnecotte were built in the 1870s and 1880s. The remainder of the lakeshore was relatively undeveloped farm property or, if rocky and steep, wild forest. Lakeside and island cottages and children's summer camps became popular only at the end of the century. The water traveler between the 1860s and 1890s either took advantage of scheduled steamer service to the major developed locations or rowed or paddled to his private destination (there were decked canoes and sailing canoes at that time but no kayaks). This situation made it possible for adventurous visitors to tour the lakes by rowboat and canoe and camp along the shore. Etiquette held that one obtained permission from the landowner to temporarily use his or her shorefront.

A diary entry by William Puffer of one such four-man rowboat trip in 1886 begins: "Arrived Weirs. Big feed at the Lakeside House. Packed and left… pulled towards Stonedam, around Pitchwood, then through Crooked River. Supper—brown bread and cocoa. Night in boat right side up. Rain! Routed out at 4:30 AM. Breakfast—hot gingerbread and rye pudding. Turned boat upside down and crawled under it all day."

Later, the rowers climbed Red Hill and met canoeists who were touring the lake in like manner. On another day, they "went to [a] farmhouse…and secured quarters in a room in their barn. Brought up our clothing, had a fire built and changed our wet for dry clothes. Had supper with the family after

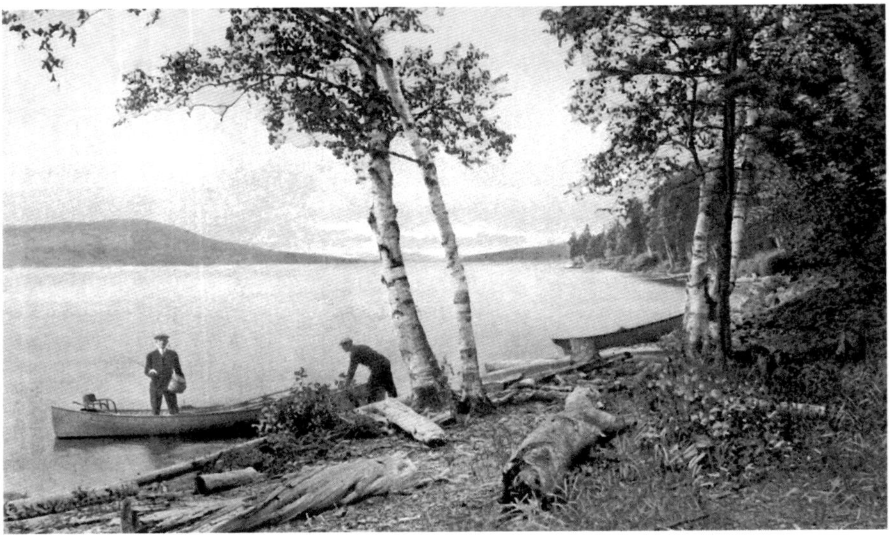

The Winnipesaukee lakeshore was mostly undeveloped until the late 1800s. *Meredith Historical Society.*

their boarders had had their supper. Unlimited milk, biscuit and cake." The rowers stopped to pick berries and bought potatoes, milk, cucumbers and dried apples from farms along the shore. They spent one month exploring and camping on Lake Winnipesaukee.[80]

Such experiences, together with stays at local hotels and boardinghouses and the back-to-nature promotions of the popular press, led summer visitors to rent or purchase shorefront property and construct more permanent camps and cottages. Another camping trend of the time was the children's summer camp. Designed first for boys, and later separately for girls, these camps were intended to give children healthful, educational and character-building experiences in natural outdoor settings.

Camp Chocorua, founded in 1881 on Squam Lake, was probably the first youth summer camp in the United States. Since then, perhaps no other part of the United States has had as many camps as the Lakes Region. The idea behind the first youth camp was an unlikely one by today's standards. Camp Chocorua founder Ernest Balch wrote that "the miserable condition of boys belonging to well-to-do families in summer hotels, considered from the point of view of their right development, set me to looking for a substitute."[81] Simply put, wealthy people who wanted to maintain their social positions needed to spend their summers at large resort hotels like the Hotel Weirs or Senter House, which catered to adults—not children. It was not socially acceptable for such families to patronize farm boardinghouses, where their children would get exercise and find interesting things to do like milking cows. So, Balch bought Chocorua Island and founded a boys' camp, where they learned outdoor skills aimed at character building, physical development and education. Camp activities included swimming, boating, fishing, baseball, land sports, cruises, singing, reading, carpentry, law court, a camp newspaper, letter-writing, cooking, charity, Sunday worship and a "liberty day" without rules.

The idea became widely popular, and by 1888, the first girls' camp had appeared, also on Squam Lake. As camps for boys led to camps for girls, so camps for wealthy children led to camps for those less privileged. In 1900, Camp Hale for boys from lower-income families of Boston's South End was founded. Camps proliferated, with many being established around Lake Winnipesaukee, and they provided opportunities for children of all income levels. Each had a distinct personality while still following the model set by Balch's Camp Chocorua.

Camp Kuwiyan for girls was located at Lovejoy Sands on Meredith Neck. In 1928, it had a massive central lodge with fireplaces, a library and function rooms. Located outdoors were wooden platforms on which the girls' sleeping tents were installed. There was a kitchen, an open-sided dining enclosure, a barn for fourteen saddle horses, a workshop with looms and handicraft equipment and a theater. At the shore were a motorboat, a war canoe, a diving float, canoes and rowboats. The girls came to Meredith by train, accompanied by their counselors, from Baltimore, Philadelphia and New York City. B. Altman & Company on New York's Fifth Avenue was the official camp outfitter. The girls' spending money was deposited in the camp's "Kuwiyan Bank," and they were given personal checks to make withdrawals, with a staff member's approval. Advice to parents was that "children visit their dentist before leaving for camp" and that "the sending of candy is discouraged, and candy will be received only in moderate quantities subject to the control of the Directors."

Many camps had religious sponsorship, as at the neighboring Lake Winnisquam camps Waldron for boys and Andover for girls, sponsored by the City Missionary Society of Boston. At Waldron and Andover, the boys and girls addressed all the staff members as "uncle" or "aunt." In 1940, the camp directors were "Uncle Cal" and "Aunt Elsa," and the camp doctor, a graduate of Yale Medical School, was "Uncle Peter." The Waldron boys made a traditional canoe camping trip from Lake Winnisquam to Lake Winnipesaukee by paddling through downtown Laconia, portaging around

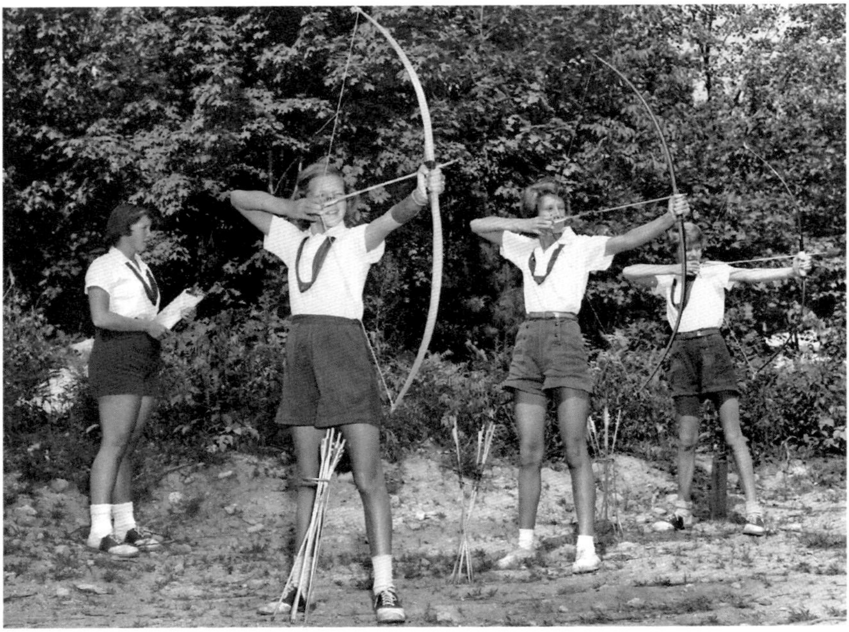

Archery at Camp Kuwiyan. There were awards for performance in each sport. *Meredith Historical Society.*

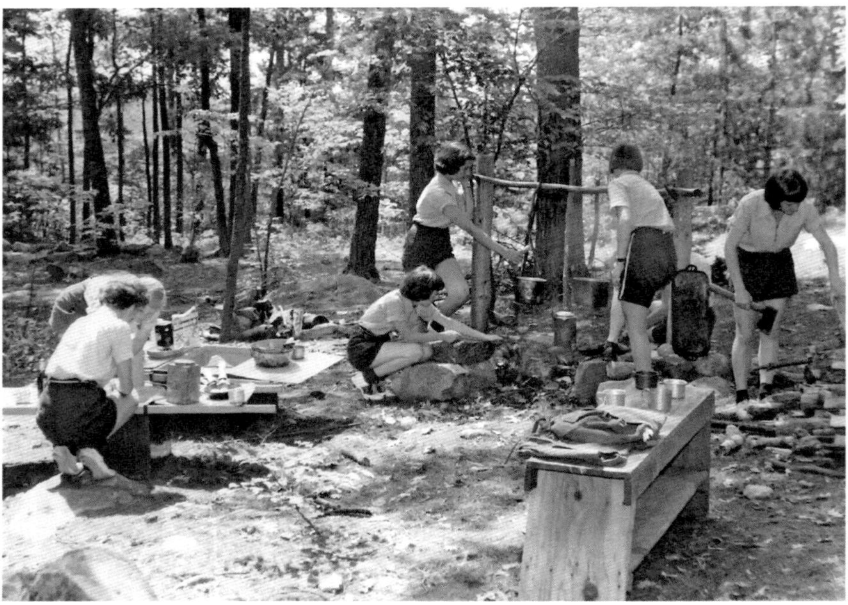

Learning techniques of outdoor cooking was another summer camp activity. *Meredith Historical Society.*

the dams. The camps' advice to parents was that "every camper should bring three or more heavy blankets (the nights are often very cold). Campers wear no underclothing with their uniform. Girls' need for underclothing will be determined by what they plan to wear at camp."

Many former campers remember Meredith because that is where they got off the train. Children from some camps marched or rode their horses in Meredith parades. Camp Waldron and Camp Andover were on the west shore of Lake Winnisquam, from which the campers hiked back into the hills and visited Meredith Center for ice cream. During the 1930s, there were thirty-three children's summer camps on Lake Winnipesaukee, with more on Lakes Winnisquam and Squam. The camp idea is still current, with Camp Nokomis for girls and Camp Lawrence for boys on Bear Island, as well as the Girl Scout's Camp Menotomy on Meredith Neck.

Chapter 20

Meredith in the News

George Fellows, the Keysers and the Winter Carnival

In the 1920s, Meredith was in the regional news, and even in the newsreels, on three different occasions. The newsreels are gone, as are most of the people, but the newspapers carried accounts of the events that we can still read.

The *Meredith News* of November 18, 1925, reported that as of that date, the man who shot and injured Ashland police chief George Dow had not been apprehended, despite the offer of a reward of $4,800, use of trained tracking dogs, woods-combing bands of armed men and state militiamen and the participation of Governor Winant in the manhunt.

George Fellows escaped the scene of the shooting, but his description was quickly broadcast on the radio and carried in the newspapers, putting everyone on the alert. This led to many reported sightings in the Meredith–Center Harbor area. A man riding in a wagon was ordered down at gunpoint, but he was not Fellows. A Center Harbor resident reported seeing a man of Fellows's description walking down a road, and authorities searched the area around the Mayo farm at Lake Waukewan, finding nothing but an open window. A suspect was chased for miles through the woods by Meredith police, who finally found him hiding behind a stone wall. He was arrested and spent the night in jail, but when Ashland officials arrived, they said that he was not Fellows. Famous Doberman Pinscher police dog Deeka was brought in on the case and led to the room where Fellows had been living, but the clever criminal had sprayed his clothing with oil of citronella, and Deeka refused to take even one whiff. The famous dog then departed for Chicago to be the mascot at the Dartmouth-Chicago football game.

A man driving near Lake Wicwas saw a man of Fellows's description walking along the road. When the driver attempted to speak to him, the man jumped a stone wall and ran into the woods. The driver related this occurrence to someone else, who, in turn, told the rural mail carrier, who told the postmaster, who told the county solicitor, who gathered a posse, including the postmaster. They discovered that someone had made a bed in the hay of a nearby barn and had left chewing tobacco juice on the floor, but Deeka was not available to follow this trail. Many other leads were investigated, and Deeka was later turned loose in Meredith, Center Harbor and Ashland, with no positive result.

A report was then received that Fellows had been sighted near Sellar's cottages, had been shot at and had fired back. This led to the sounding of the Meredith fire alarm, the combing of the woods and roads by hundreds of armed men and the calling up of some one hundred members of the state militia, plus a militia motor contingent. The militia disembarked at Meredith's Boston & Maine railroad station and took over the waiting room, where the large stove was fired up to keep them warm overnight. Governor Winant arrived to join General Howard and militia officers at their headquarters in the station's baggage room, where the governor briefed reporters arriving from around the state. The militiamen and more trained dogs then fanned out over the wooded hills, while the governor inspected the roads, accompanied by Meredith's Leslie French, a noted hunter, trapper and guide. Nothing was found, and it was concluded that Fellows was no longer in the area, whereupon the *Meredith News* printed an anonymous poet's lines:

They searched the woods by the Sellar's camps/But the bandit wasn't there
They hailed the travelers and stopped the tramps/No bandit was near to care
The soldiers came and a squad of police/Oh where was the bandit, where?
They expected to nab him as slick as grease/With an army I do declare!
Oh, where's the bandit? No one can tell/He may be departed, perhaps to—well,
He has in Concord a prison cell/But the bandit isn't there

According to accounts in the *Manchester Union* and the *Meredith News*, a heart-wrenching scene took place on a day in late November 1928: the eviction of the Keyser family from their home, today known as the "Towle House," on Route 25 between Meredith and Center Harbor. Sheriff Frederick Elliott of Laconia, Deputy Charles Whiting of Meredith and assisting officers

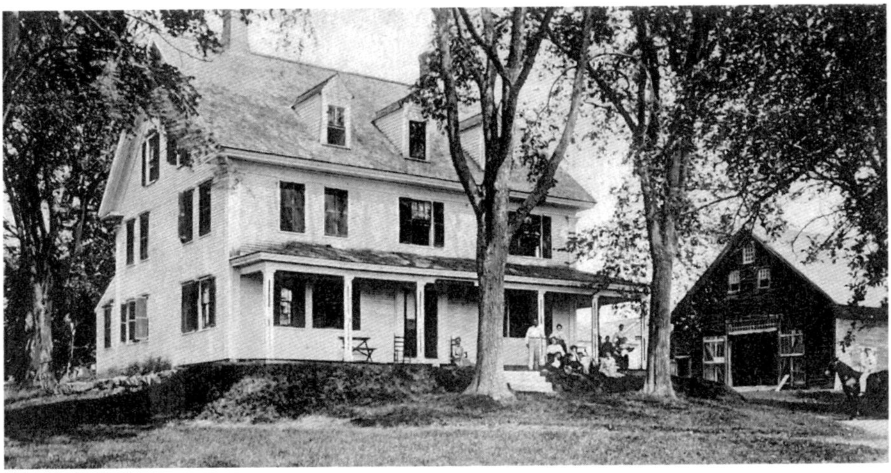

The Keyser family's Mountain View House. *Meredith Historical Society.*

enforced an eviction, which was the result of the property having been sold at auction to Henry B. Clow of Laconia. The five Keyser family members occupying the house had disagreed legally among themselves on the question of dividing the estate that they had inherited from their parents. This caused the court to sell the property at auction in order to divide the proceeds among them. The Keyser family had owned the house and farm for some fifty years, operating it as a popular tourist inn under the name of Mountain View House. The unresolved dispute among them and a misunderstanding of the law caused Arthur and Charles Keyser; their sisters, Emma and Sadie; and Sadie's husband, James Nave, to be conducted out their front door to a waiting audience of neighbors, reporters, photographers and movie men.

A sheriff's crew removed their possessions: beds, bedding, rugs, chairs, tables, clothing and the contents of the cellar and attic, piling them on the lawn. They next emptied the barn of thirty cattle, two horses, two pigs, sixty chickens, potatoes, preserves and tools—everything but the hay. While this was going on, the household's boy, six-year-old Walter Nave, came home from school to find his books and toys in the front yard.

Upon stepping out the door, Charles, who had lived there for forty-eight years, broke down and sobbed, "I've worked so hard to build up this farm, I can't leave it now." His sister Sadie comforted him, saying, "I don't want my share of the estate. You take it. You deserve it." The *Meredith News* reported that he told the sheriff, who was not enjoying this unpleasant job in the least,

"You might just as well kill me." Onlookers, including those who had just emptied the house, were noticeably touched. The family was then driven in police cars to the house of John Willey, a neighbor who had offered to take them in. Snow fell on their things that were piled up on the lawn.

The internal divisions in the Keyser family were now at an end, and other people were taking steps to help. Purchaser Henry Clow, who had witnessed the eviction, said that he did not know the circumstances when he bought the property and that he was too old and his time here too short for him to try to do wrong to anybody. The Meredith selectmen consulted county officials, who suggested that the Keysers request a conservator, and Daniel Eaton was appointed to that role. Eaton met with Clow, who offered to give the property back and help the Keysers financially. Three days after receiving their eviction notice, the Keysers were back in their house. Neighbors and Mr. Eaton were helping to move the furnishings back inside. Even the heavy kitchen and parlor stoves had been taken out to the yard and had to be put back in place. James and Sadie and their son, Walter, would not stay but would receive Sadie's share of the estate in cash to enable them to settle on their own. Emma, Charles and Arthur would run the farm, and Arthur would resume his milk route once the evicted cows were returned from their stay in a Center Harbor barn.

Freda Perkins Cronin, who grew up on Meredith's Reservoir Road, wrote in a 2013 letter that she "was ten years old and remember how bad my parents felt for the Keysers, and they brought Walter to our home to live. He did not have many clothes with him. My mother asked me if I would mind if he wore my brand new flannel pajamas. So these new PJ's were his. He walked to school with me. Later on, I was to meet him [again]; he grew up to be a handsome man."

A few years later, the sixteen-room Keyser house and the 165-acre farm was again offered for sale. It was purchased by people from Massachusetts, and the *News* reported that hay was again being cut in its fields. This house has seen more changes since then, including the disappearance of its impressive one-hundred- by forty-foot roadside barn, removal of its front porch and a recent remodeling into office space.

"The Carnival! Where can the News find words to express its pleasure over the success of this event, which was laughed at when first...mentioned." So wrote the *Meredith News* on February 11, 1925. Meredith put its heart and soul into its first Winter Carnival, organized by the chamber of commerce. Planned to run for three days in early February, the carnival was widely publicized, including ads in all the theater programs in Boston. Businesses contributed prizes, and residents served on committees and subcommittees for each event. A Carnival Information Bureau was opened and staffed, with its own telephone number: 50. Meredith's only hotel was closed for the season, so an ambitious lodging program was launched involving house parties and the opening of summer camps. Hotels at the Weirs and Center Harbor benefited considerably. Churches offered suppers, as did the Grange, which featured sliced tongue and ham on its menu. The Meredith Library was kept open for the convenience of visitors. The *Boston Globe*, the *Boston Transcript*, the *Post*, the *Manchester Union* and the *Christian Science Monitor* were contacted and sent reporters.

The carnival started with a bonfire fueled by 150 empty tar barrels, followed by a confetti fight. There was a torchlight procession and a baby parade, with the babies riding in forty-one elaborate floats—airplanes, flowers, puritans, cowboys, gypsies, valentines, a snowman and a sled pulled by six boys dressed as sled dogs and harnessed together. On the ice of Meredith Bay, there were motorcycle, automobile and horse races watched by more than one thousand spectators. Steve Collins rode a ski motorcycle he had built, winning one race, but crashing into a snowbank in another. Teams from the New Hampton Literary Institute and Meredith High School played a baseball game on snowshoes in which one player lost two teeth and

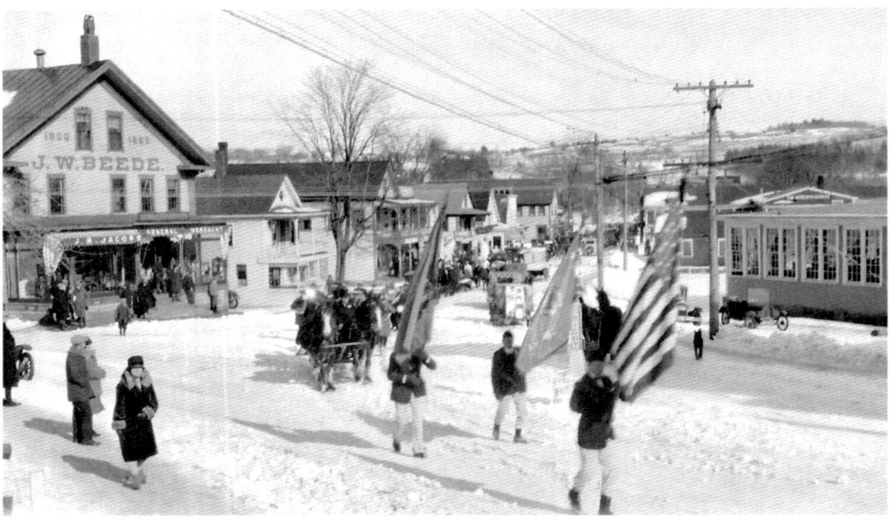

A Winter Carnival parade passing Plymouth Street on its way to Post Office Square (today's Historical Society Museum), 1920s. *Meredith Public Library.*

another was cut on the head. Both were attended to by Meredith's venerable Dr. Hawkins, who was also one of the carnival's organizers.

There were ski, snowshoe and skate races over various distances and courses, including an obstacle course and relays—for girls, boys under fourteen years old and boys over fourteen. Six dog teams and drivers ran a thirty-two-mile sled dog race from Meredith to Tamworth one day, returning to Meredith the next. One team was helped when a fast-moving goat entered the course and was pursued by the dogs for two miles. Walter Channing, driving seven dogs, won the race in a time of four hours, twenty-two minutes. Two female drivers ran the race, with Caryl Peabody and her team of four huskies taking third place. Engraved silver cups were awarded to the winners of these races.

Indoors at the town hall, there were moving pictures, a concert, the procession and crowning of the Carnival Queen and a dress ball. The queen was Doris Moulton, a Meredith telephone operator, who received more than 1,500,000 votes. Second was Elsie Greenwood with more than 1,400,000 (the carnival organizers made the mistake of giving people 100 votes for each purchase of one dollar or more, and customers of Meredith businesses could vote for the Carnival Queen with each purchase of one dollar or more). More than one thousand people attended Doris Moulton's coronation ceremony, which included a procession led by two trumpeters wearing capes and plumes, ladies-in-waiting, train-bearers and a crown carried on a purple cushion. Ms. Moulton wore a custom-made white crepe

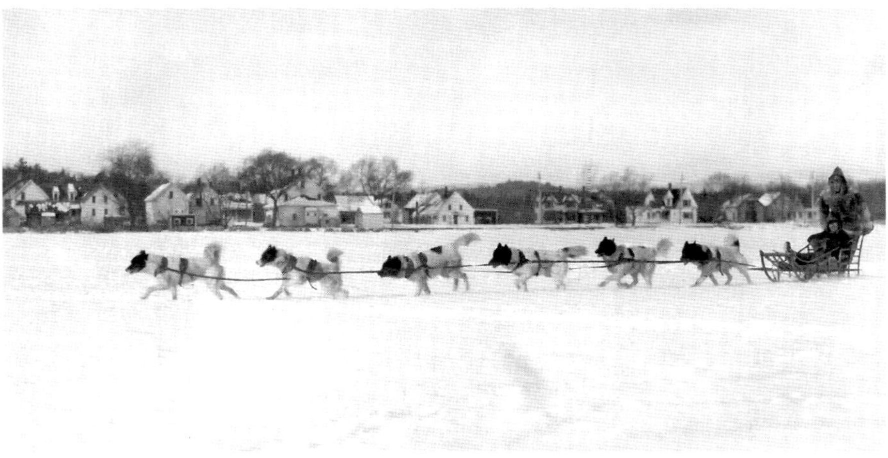

This postcard of the Meredith dog team driven by Percy Estes was the most popular souvenir of the 1925 Winter Carnival. *Meredith Public Library.*

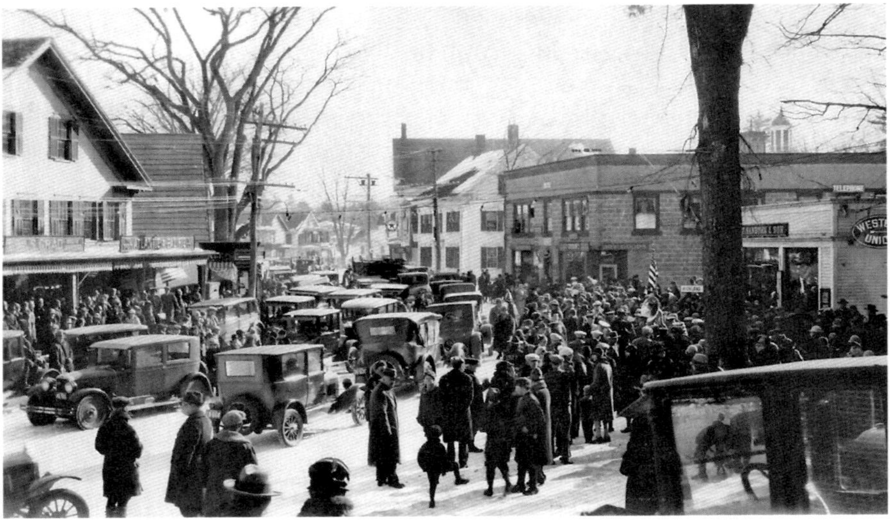

Meredith's Main Street bustled during the Winter Carnival. *Meredith Public Library.*

gown contributed by Madame Elliott of Boston and a purple velvet robe with ermine trimming donated by the Meredith Casket Company. She was given a pair of Queen Quality shoes, and her official photograph appeared on the front page of the *Meredith News*.

Souvenir carnival buttons showing the "Old Man of the Mountain" and the Meredith Latchkey were available for purchase, as were commemorative booklets, but the most popular item was a postcard photograph of the Meredith dog team—471 postcards were sold. Many more winter carnivals were to follow this successful first one.

Chapter 21

The Great Hurricane of 1938

There are those in Meredith who remember the great Hurricane of 1938, and there are reminders of that storm even today. Moving forward at 60 to 70 miles per hour and packing winds of more than 110 miles per hour, the storm hit New England virtually unannounced on September 21, 1938. The eye of the storm followed a path up the Connecticut River Valley and then veered northwest to pass over Burlington, with the strongest winds on the east side of the storm battering southern and central New Hampshire. The ground was already saturated and softened from prior heavy rain, and the very fast forward movement of the storm added to the force of the storm's own cyclonic winds. A hurricane of this magnitude had not struck New England since 1869, and its impact was devastating. Some 15 million acres of trees, about one-third of the forest, were uprooted or snapped, and it is estimated that New Hampshire lost half of its white pines.

After the disaster response of clearing roads and railroads, restoring electric and telephone service and repairing or demolishing damaged buildings, thoughts turned to the danger of forest fires in the tracts of downed and drying trees. Two depression-era agencies, the Civilian Conservation Corps (CCC) and the Works Progress Administration (WPA), put their manpower and organizational resources into the clean-up. The National Forest Service put tracts of downed trees in the White Mountain National Forest out to bid to loggers, who would conduct salvage logging. A new agency, the Northeastern Timber Salvage Administration, was created to make productive use of as much of the downed forest as possible. This included

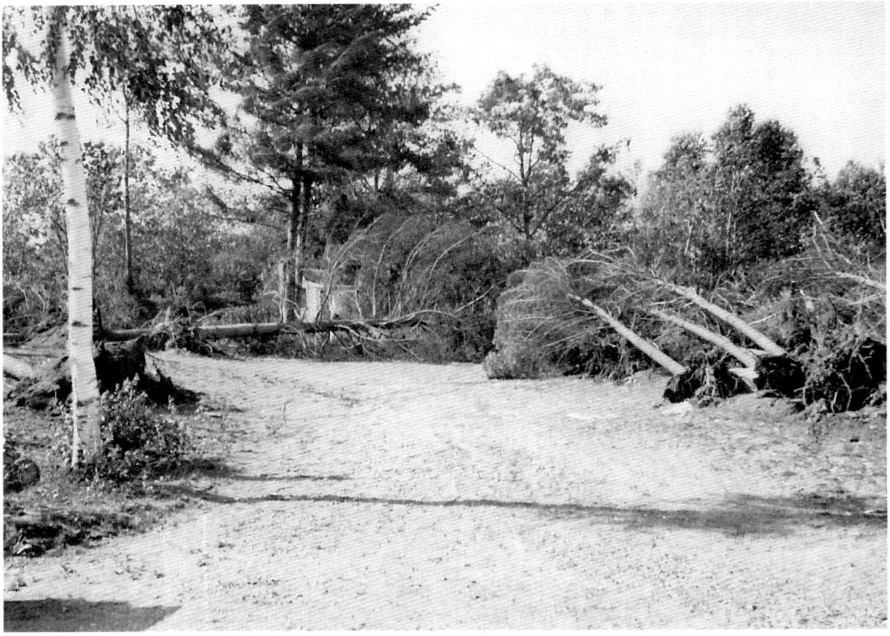

Big, top-heavy white pine trees were uprooted or snapped by the 1938 hurricane. *Meredith Historical Society.*

not just logging the downed trees but also building sawmills, setting price controls in the glutted forest products market and storing salvaged timber in ponds and lakes until it could be processed. Surplus timber had to be submerged in Lake Wicwas and near Stonedam Island in Meredith, as well as Little's, White Oak and Red Hill Ponds in Sandwich, to prevent insect damage. The Northeastern Timber Salvage Administration saved woodlot owners from ruin. By September 1939, it had paid New Hampshire timber owners for more than 319 million board feet.

The storm had not uniformly mowed down the forest; it had spared sheltered pockets, while it hit more exposed portions with a force that uprooted, snapped, splintered and smashed the trees, leaving not even enough room for a person to plant a foot on the ground. Ridge tops and slopes facing southeast were the hardest hit, and ridges were the least likely to be reached by salvage loggers. To deal with the multi-year forest fire risk, emergency fire towers were built to supplement those already in place around the area.

The hurricane also did much damage in the towns and villages, as accounts of the time reveal. The *Laconia Democrat* of September 23 reported that "martial law was proclaimed in New Hampshire as an army of WPA workers, volunteers, state police and coastguardsmen joined in rescue and rehabilitation work." Huge trees fell on buildings and across roads, taking power and telephone lines down. The Laconia district telephone manager estimated that some two thousand poles were down. The steeple of the church across from the Laconia railroad station was blown down, damaging the station and crushing Chet Randlett's car. Radio station WLNH's 150-foot broadcast tower was toppled, and the station was out of service for more than twenty-four hours, until a temporary antenna was attached to a pine tree. Amateur radio operator Neil Sheeley of Franklin stayed at his set until midnight the day after the storm, relaying messages for Laconia and points north.

Railroad service was halted because of trees across the tracks and many washouts. The manager of the Laconia Western Union telegraph office drove to Concord on the second day after the storm with almost seventy-five telegrams to be sent on from there. Laconia and Meredith's postmasters were obliged to do the same, carrying mail that normally went by train. A view was opened from the Laconia airport, then off Parade Road, where destruction of a pine grove allowed downtown landmarks to be seen. Many barns were destroyed—one resident's was "pancaked" just seconds before he was to enter it. Weirs Boulevard was a scene of particular destruction, with summer camps demolished "like kindling wood." After the storm, traffic to the Weirs was as heavy as during the summer, due to people driving there to see the damage.

Children's summer camps, which were typically a group of buildings under tall pines at the lakeshore, were extensively damaged. At east-facing Camp Passaconaway on Bear Island, "upended tree roots stood as high as one story buildings [and] buildings were crushed and many of the remaining furnishings were destroyed."[82] Luckily, the camping season was over, so the camps were empty. East-facing shores, such as Lake Shore Park on Lake Winnipesaukee and Long Point on Squam Lake, were hardest hit. The well-known Piscopo pine grove on Lake Winnisquam was leveled. The grove "looked as if someone had pushed each tree over." At the Hodsdon farm on Route 3, now Picnic Rock farm, some 1 million board feet of mature white pine was lost and only about half of that salvaged.

Across Meredith, many buildings were damaged, especially roofs and windows. Meredith Neck was hardest hit, with many trees down. The residential streets in Meredith Village, lined by fine old maples and elms, were not greatly affected, nor was the "Old Oak" at Scenic Park. There was fallen tree damage to homes and uprooted tree damage to sidewalks.

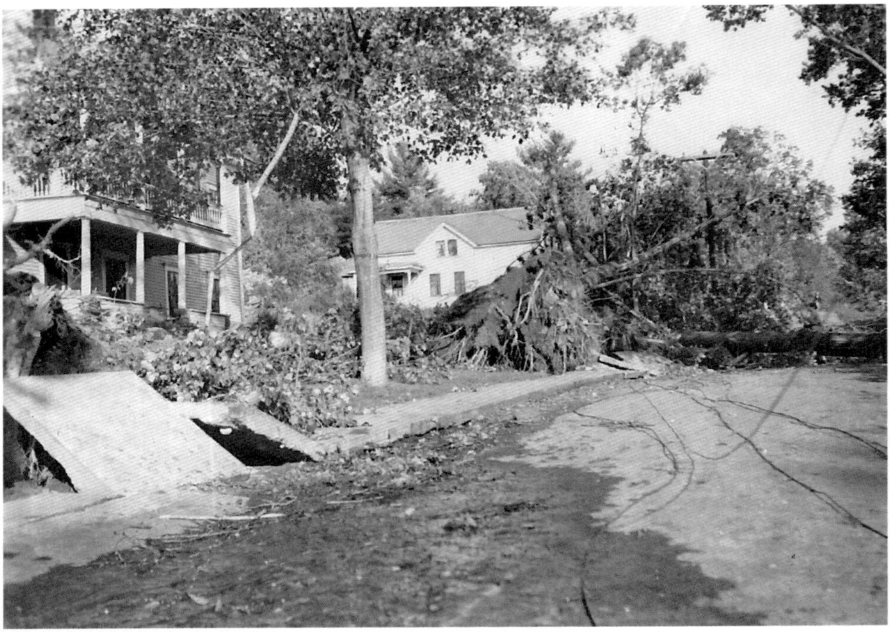

Village homes and sidewalks were damaged by downed and uprooted trees. *Meredith Historical Society.*

Power and telephone lines were torn down, but electric service was restored to much of the village center by late the next day. The *Meredith* News noted that most of the trees that were uprooted were "solid and firm."

Virtually all rural roads were blocked, and many were washed out. Clearing them—with axes and crosscut saws, not chainsaws—was the first priority. Harold Wyatt remembered the Meredith road agent telling him "to get back home, get our tools and anyone who wanted to work and do what we could to get everyone a way out." In the aftermath of the Great Depression, there were plenty of men anxious to earn the money. Chemung Road was washed out for nearly one thousand feet, twelve to fourteen feet deep. He explained today's lack of stone walls in some places: repair crews had to roll the stones into the washed-out roads for fill—an enduring reminder of September 1938.[83]

Chapter 22

Meredith Life in the Early 1900s

A widely known Meredith farm in 1912 was Edward Wiggin's on Parade and Reservoir Roads, which had one thousand acres overall, with about seventy acres in crops and the rest in pasture, hayfields and timber. The eighty-four-foot-long barn held a herd of forty Shorthorn Durham milk cows and a prize bull. There were seven yoke of oxen, plus Merino sheep, Berkshire hogs and two pairs of horses. The large, roomy farmhouse, with a view of the mountains, was run as a summer boardinghouse for a dozen vacationing guests by daughters Florence and Ethel and other helpers, while son Hollis supervised the farm work. The farm's apple orchard produced some two hundred barrels a year from old trees, with new trees just beginning to bear. The fields yielded six hundred bushels of corn for the silo, as well as potatoes and vegetables for the farmhouse kitchen.[84]

The large Wiggin house, barn, silo and outbuildings were destroyed by the town in the mid-1930s because they were too close to the town reservoir. Just stone walls and a few apple trees remain of this model farm property, which is now Meredith's Waukewan Highlands Park.

During the 1920s and 1930s, a major Meredith attraction was Pinnacle Park on Meredith Neck. Originally developed as a zoo by Meredith businessman and farm owner Charles Roberts and open during the summer from 9:00

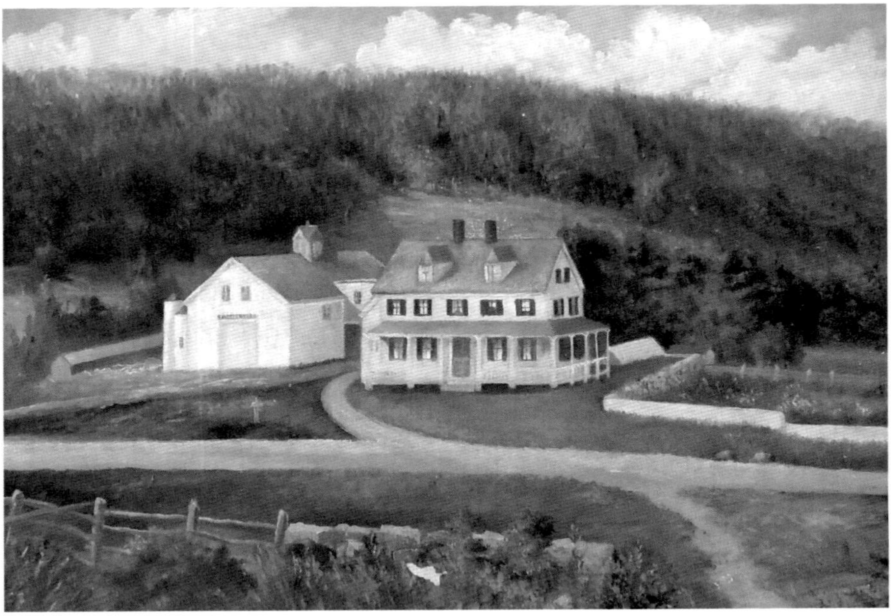

The Wiggin house and farm buildings once stood on Parade Road at today's Waukewan Park. *Meredith Historical Society.*

a.m. to 7:00 p.m., the park in the 1920s featured bears; silver, red and gray foxes; baboons; monkeys; raccoons; mink; and a "wild cat from Africa." The *Meredith News* noted that visitors found squirrels, Angora rabbits, jack rabbits, prairie dogs, guinea pigs, spotted deer, a skunk, a donkey, two billy goats and even an alligator. There were "the only blue pigs on exhibition in this country…buffaloes, Aberdeen Angus cattle" and "golden and silver pheasants, wild and domestic geese, peacocks, foreign pigeons and doves, [and] many prize-winning species of fowls." The zoo property was also home to Meredith's "thoroughbred Eskimo dog team," which competed in the annual Winter Carnival. Helping to care for the chained or penned animals, each labeled with its common-usage name, were Charles Roberts's daughter, Frances, and son, Charles Jr. Frances also was in charge of collecting the admission fee of twenty-five cents per adult, with children under fifteen years of age admitted free.

Charles Roberts, who was an avid collector, also erected a large exhibition building to house items of historical interest. Here were displayed "antiques used by the first settlers," "Indian relics" found near Endicott Rock at the Weirs, a doctor's medicine bag, china, prints and samplers, wooden furniture, chests, wool and flax spinning wheels, farm tools and braided rugs—some of them for sale. Also in this building were an early vintage Pierce-Arrow automobile on loan from Lew Kelley of Center Harbor, a horse-drawn chaise, a Meredith hand-pump fire engine and a use-worn 1850 Concord coach that had carried guests at Center Harbor's Senter House hotel. This coach was then on loan from the Sandwich Historical Society but at that time had not yet been restored.

The road to the zoo continued up to "The Pinnacle," where there was room to park cars, walk through a gate and climb to the top of the summit rock. From this point, a stunning 360-degree view was to be had, including the entire basin of Lake Winnipesaukee, with its more than two hundred

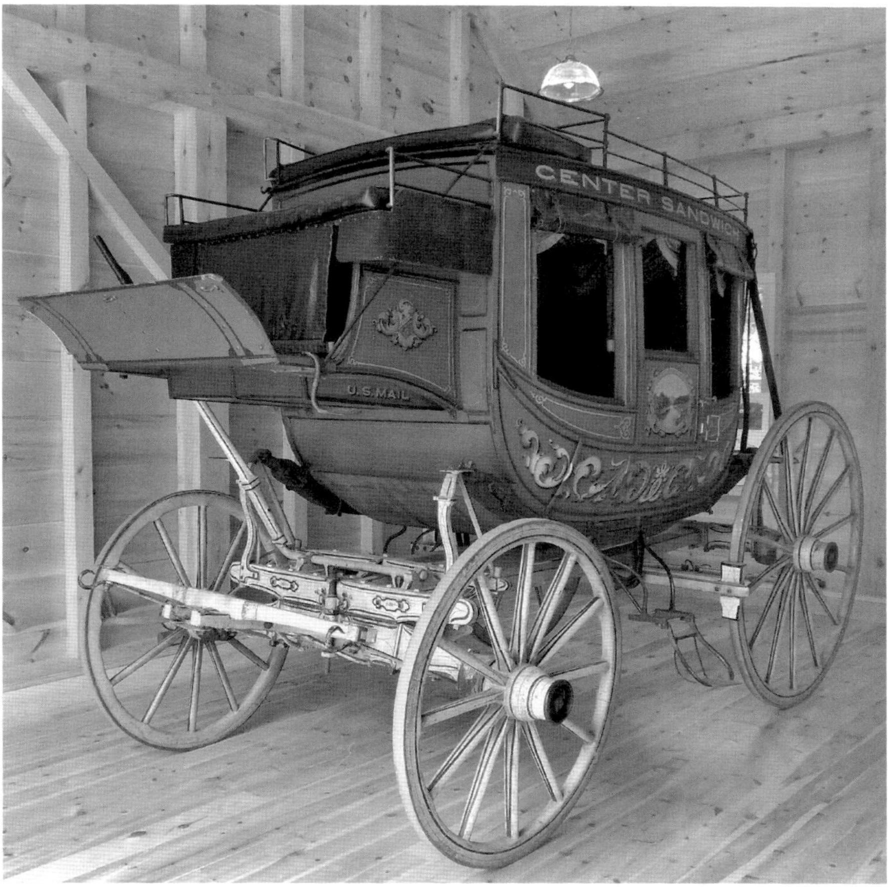

The Sandwich Historical Society's Concord coach, now restored, was on display at Meredith's Pinnacle Park during the 1920s and 1930s. *Daniel Heyduk.*

islands, and the Belknap, Ossipee and White Mountains. This view was considered to be superior to those from Mount Major, the Ossipees or Red Hill because it placed the viewer in the center of the bowl of lake and mountains. In winter, ski trails starting from near this point allowed one to ski down to, and out onto, Lake Winnipesaukee.

Pinnacle Park entertainment was not limited to the zoo. One day in October 1926, a monkey escaped while returning from a visit to the Rochester Fair and went on a tour of Meredith Village. The monkey entered through the open door of Gus Moscardini's Meredith Fruit Company and began to scamper around, grabbing and eating fruit. In the crowded, fruit-filled space, the agile monkey evaded capture by Charles Roberts and other pursuers and dealt a discouraging blow to a pursuing dog before being snared by a leg-holding lasso wielded by Charles Weeks.

The hurricane of September 1938 caused much destruction on Meredith Neck and extensively damaged the animal enclosures at Pinnacle Park. This led Charles Roberts to dismantle the zoo and the historical exhibit, donating in 1939 a substantial collection of historical items to the Sandwich Historical Society, where they may be seen today. Also at that time, he returned the Concord coach and chaise to that historical society—also on display there today.

Most Meredith children went to one-room schools during the 1800s, but they also did so in the first half of the twentieth century. One such school was in Meredith Center at the corner of Livingston and Meredith Center Roads. In the mid-1920s, this one-room, one-teacher school had more than twenty students from families living in the Center and on the surrounding farms. Its only light came through the windows, and it was heated in winter by a wood stove. Drinking water was carried in by hand from the cement watering trough across the street. There was an adjoining playground with swings and a merry-go-round.

On one winter lunch break, a group of boys went sledding down from the top of Livingston Road on a "traverse" made of two short sleds connected by a long board. The roads then were not plowed but "rolled," and the packed surface made for considerable speed. They passed the school, heading down Meredith Center Road toward the mills, but failed to make the right turn to cross the old bridge—now Sirles Road. Instead, they plowed through the door of Joe Smith's store—located where the "new" bridge is today—and

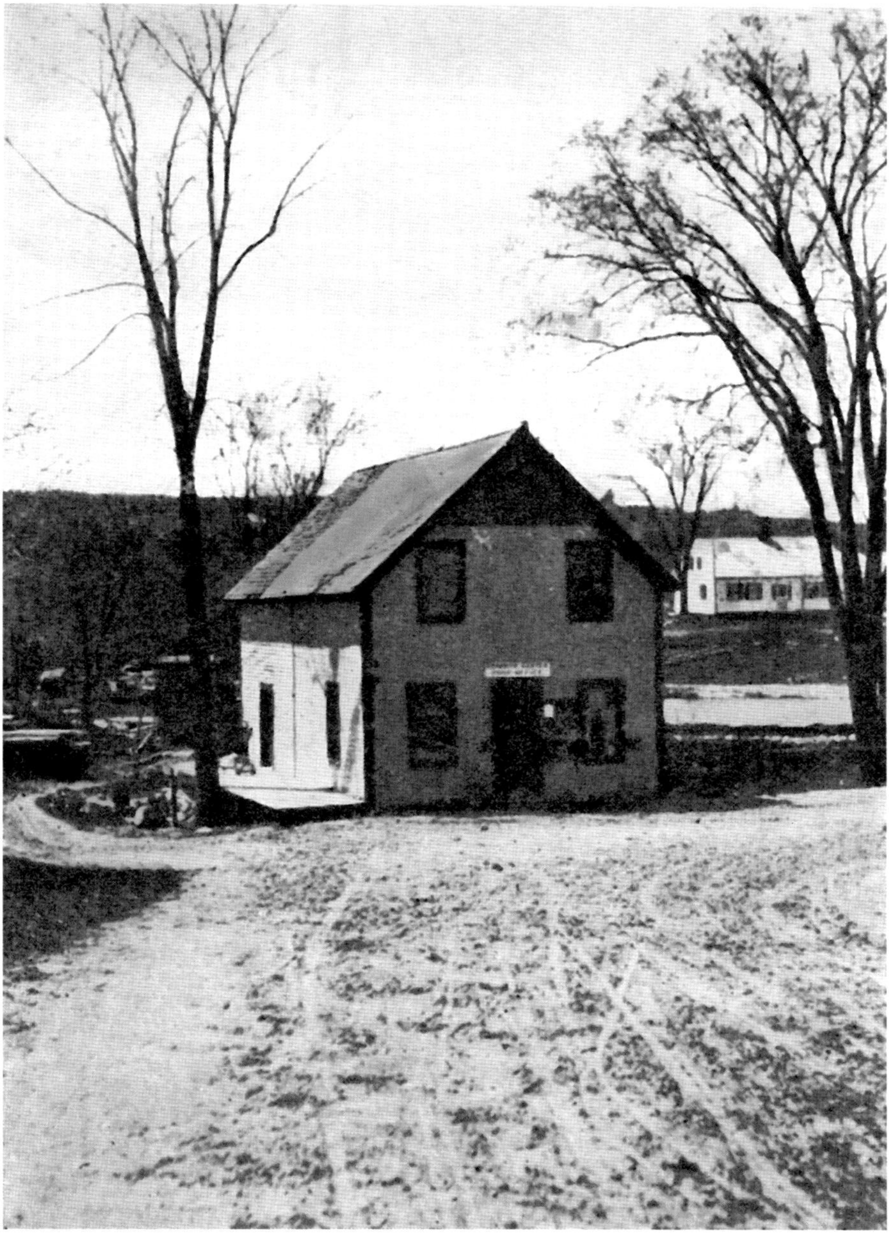

Joe Smith's store and post office stood at today's intersection of Meredith Center and Sirles Roads. *Meredith Historical Society.*

hit the stove, disconnecting it from the stovepipe and filling the floor with soot. Mrs. Ora Dow, who minded the store, ordered them to fix and clean everything before returning to school.[85]

The cement watering trough, built by Fred Sanborn in 1913 and used by horses and schoolchildren, is still at the corner of Corliss Hill and Meredith Center Roads, in front of the Lake Wicwas Grange, which was built in 1930. The store the boys sledded into is gone, replaced by the current Meredith Center Road bridge over Mill Brook, but the old road and bridge that they tried to turn into is still there. Meredith Center's mills and dam were replaced by the new road and bridge, but the mill's foundations can still be seen. The millpond is gone, but today, beavers have partially restored it with their own dam upstream of the old bridge.

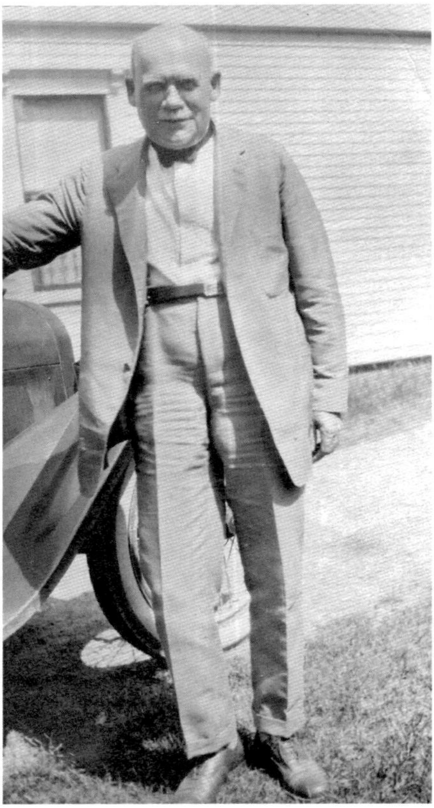

Dr. Frederick Hawkins practiced medicine in Meredith for more than forty years. *Meredith Historical Society.*

The early twentieth century was still the era of the country doctor who made house calls. In Meredith, from the late 1880s to the 1940s, that was Frederick Hawkins. He was born in Meredith in 1861 and was orphaned after his father, William, died in the Civil War in 1863 and his mother, Ellen, died six years later. He attended local schools, including the Tilton School, and worked in his uncle's shoe factory in Portland, Maine. After completing medical school in Philadelphia, Dr. Hawkins returned to Meredith and married twenty-three-year-old Geneva Moses in 1889.

As was the custom, he established an office in his home, where patients could drop in. Dr. Hawkins's advertisement in the *Meredith News*, unchanged for decades, simply read, "Office in residence," without any telephone number or even the address (corner of Main and Waukewan Streets). In addition to office hours, he regularly made house calls, sometimes at a distance and in terrible weather. Dr. Hawkins also covered Center Harbor during his first years of practice, and he remembered being "on duty all day in Meredith, a hasty supper, and then rush to Center Harbor [by horse and buggy] to work there until midnight."

Dr. Hawkins also recalled that "it wasn't uncommon…for the average country doctor when on long trips to be obliged to ask for lodging at some farm house on the way. Sometimes he'd arrive so exhausted because of having to shovel a path for his horse that he was forced to rest before digging into his medical bag."[86] Many house calls were for childbirth, which commonly occurred at home and for which the doctor remained until the baby arrived. Because pharmacies were few and difficult for rural patients to reach, doctors carried a large supply of medicines, preparing and dispensing them as required. Country doctors eventually got automobiles, but rural roads were not plowed in winter until well into the 1920s.

Dr. Hawkins's house is today a bed-and-breakfast inn, a modern version of the many vacation boardinghouses of Meredith's past.

When railroads provided vital transportation for the Lakes Region in the late nineteenth and early twentieth centuries, disruptions to service affected not just passengers but also farmers, businesses and the mail. The railroad right-of-way was narrow, easily blocked or cut and could be serviced only via the existing track. The rails were smooth-surfaced, as were the wheels of the locomotives, so mobility could be lost on uphill grades or if ice (or even wet leaves) covered the tracks. Switches and signals were vital, but they could break or become frozen if they were not constantly maintained.

A storm on Saturday, March 6, 1920, began with rain, which froze on the rails and then was followed by heavy snow. The evening northbound passenger train left Meredith station but became stranded before reaching Winona. Passengers in the several cars were forced to spend the night on the train, but word of their predicament reached Meredith, and the town mobilized the next morning. The *Meredith News* reported that "Meredith turned out en masse. The preachers left their pulpits and the males of the entire community went to the scene and shoveled for hours, finally digging the engine and cars out of the ice." At the same time, groups of girls on snowshoes carried food to the passengers. When the train was finally cleared, the crew managed to back it up to Meredith station on Sunday night, where the women of the town had brought "hot coffee, sandwiches, doughnuts and other edibles" to feed the passengers. Since rail service was still disrupted, Meredith families took passengers home with them, where they stayed until the following Tuesday, when the trains began to run again at noon.

Meredith Village had several important mills in the early 1900s. After Sam Hodgson's hosiery mill burned in 1889, the Hall brothers built the Meredith Linen Mill on the same site, using Waukewan Canal's water power. The mill used no American-grown flax to make its linen. All of its flax was imported from Europe and brought into Meredith by rail. The linen mill overcame competition from European mills to produce competitive, high-quality linen toweling for the U.S. market. By 1913, it was producing 2 million yards of linen towel fabric annually and was Meredith's major employer for the next three decades of the twentieth century.

There were several woodworking mills in the village. The Meredith Shook and Lumber Company was started in 1886 by Nathan Wadleigh and later sold to the Dodge & Bliss Company of New Jersey. It employed some sixty people in the manufacture of mouldings, frames and "shooks" from which boxes were assembled. Located on the Winnipesaukee lakeshore, the company used the lake for towing logs by steam tug or over the ice by oxen to its sawmill. It went out of operation in about 1912, but the buildings remained vacant and unused into the 1920s, eventually becoming the site of St. Charles Catholic Church. The George H. Clark Company, located at the Winnipesaukee lakeshore, had been producing woodwork—including box shooks, hosiery boards and cabinet work—since 1866.[87] It employed some thirty-five people up to its closure in 1926. Another woodworking business was the Meredith Casket Company, which shipped caskets by rail to a wide market.[88]

The site of the Meredith Linen Mill is today's Mill Falls Marketplace, where the water of the Waukewan Canal still flows. Meredith's lakeshore, once occupied by lumber mills and the Catholic church, is now the Church Landing complex, the Meredith town docks and Hesky Park.

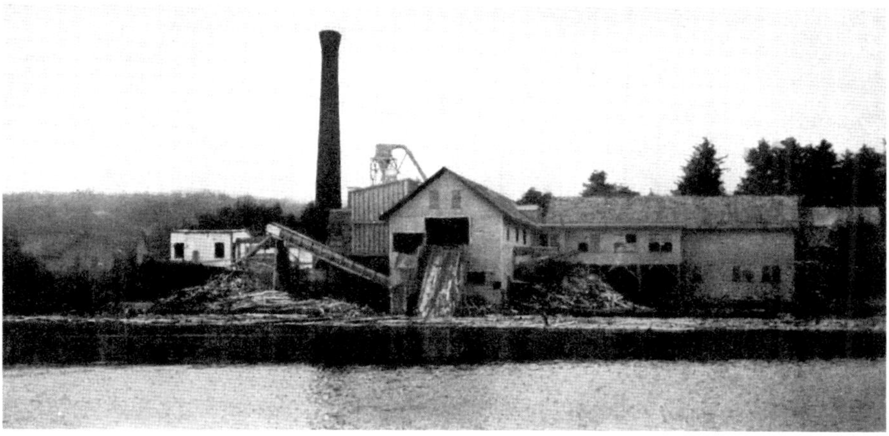

The Meredith Shook and Lumber Company occupied the lakefront where the Church Landing complex is today. *Meredith Historical Society.*

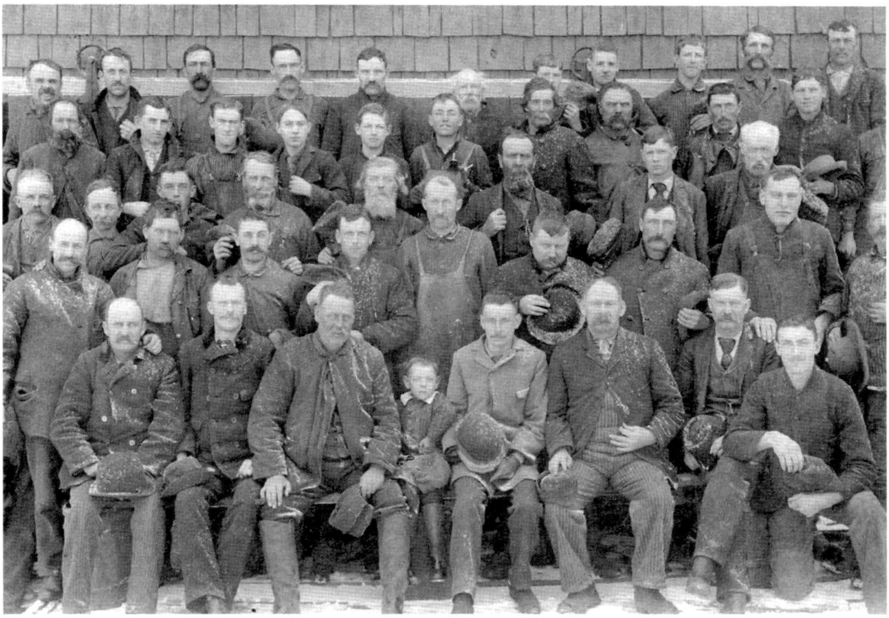

Workers at the Shook and Lumber Company sat with their hats off in the snow for this group photo. *Meredith Historical Society.*

Edgar Maloon began manufacturing wheelbarrows in the late 1800s, and in 1909, that business was purchased by Frank Prescott, who built the Prescott Lumber Company where the current lumberyard is today. The company employed forty workers and produced specialty lumber, box shooks and wheelbarrows, which were shipped out in large numbers from the neighboring B&M rail station. On a cold, windy night in February 1940, the Prescott Lumber building burned, consuming five hundred wheelbarrows and tons of construction material. Frank Prescott, then seventy years old, vowed to his employees that he would rebuild, and he did.[89]

Afterword

The story of the land and people of today's Meredith has taken many twists and turns. Native Americans pursued the same way of life for generations at a stretch but still faced periodic changes in climate, warfare, lean times, new developments in subsistence and changes in population. Then, from 1600 onward, few children of either Native American or European descent lived quite the same lives as had their mothers and fathers. Epidemics, international trade and warfare caused rapid change. Clearing of the land and much of its native wildlife; small-scale farming giving way to the sheep boom and then to abandonment of the pastures; industrialization; population growth and decline; changing village life; the arrival and disappearance of the railroad, steamboats and the big hotels; farms becoming boardinghouses and vacation homes; disappearing mills; growth in lakeshore second homes and recreation; and the renewal of the hospitality business were all major shifts affecting people's lives. Families, schools, churches, music, associations, entertainment, the law and government changed as well.

This history stops with the beginning of "living memory" in the 1930s. There are many people who vividly remember the time since the 1930s or who heard about it from their parents and grandparents. There are scrapbooks, diaries, photo collections, town reports, newspapers and books cataloguing this time. The Meredith Historical Society and the Meredith Public Library have some of these and will have more as time passes. These records are important for future historians and will become more so with time.

Notes

Chapter 1

1. For more, see Boisvert, "Decline of the Ice Age"; Dorion, "Decline of the Ice Age"; Potter, "New Hampshire's Landscape and Environment"; Thompson, "Decline of the Ice Age"; Caduto, *Time Before New Hampshire*; Starbuck, *Archeology of New Hampshire*.
2. More from archaeological evidence can be found in Caduto, *Time Before New Hampshire*, and Starbuck, *Archeology of New Hampshire*.
3. For a complete description of Native American canoe craft, see Adney and Chapelle, *Bark Canoes and Skin Boats*.
4. Woodland is the Native American culture that Europeans found when they reached New England. See Starbuck, *Archeology of New Hampshire*, for an archaeological description and Caduto, *Time Before New Hampshire*, for a description that includes folk history.

Chapter 2

5. Merrill, *History of Carroll County*.
6. Lyford, *History of the Town of Canterbury*.
7. Hurd, *History of Merrimack and Belknap Counties*.
8. Ibid.

9. Blaisdell, *Meredith Parade*.
10. Ford, *Colonial Ebenezer Smith*.
11. Vadeboncoeur et al., "Comparison of Presettlement."

Chapter 3

12. Garvin and Garvin, *On the Road North of Boston*.
13. Hurd, *History of Merrimack and Belknap Counties*.
14. Wyatt, *Road Histories of Meredith*.
15. Garvin and Garvin, *On the Road North of Boston*.
16. Blaisdell, *Meredith Parade*.
17. United States Postal Service, *United States Postal Service*.
18. Scheiber, "Coach, Wagon, and Motor-Truck Manufacture."
19. Article by Edgar H. Maloon, *Meredith News*, February 6, 1924. My clarifications are in brackets.

Chapter 4

20. Wilcomb, "Meredith's Old Almanac Maker."
21. This house was later sold and moved to Route 25, near the Meredith–Center Harbor town line, where a historical marker now stands.
22. Heald, *New Hampshire Learnin' Days*.
23. Heald, *Reminisce the Valley*.
24. Actual 1816 weather observations in quotes are from Joshua Lane, Sanbornton town clerk.

Chapter 5

25. Wyatt, *Panfull of Knotholes*.

Chapter 6

26. Parks, "New England Textile Mill Villages."
27. See Pickering, "Meredith School History."
28. Article by Mary Blake Benson, the *Meredith News*, July 29, 1930.

29. Maloon, "Glancing Over Meredith's Past."
30. Hurd, *History of Merrimack and Belknap Counties*.

CHAPTER 7

31. Woodford, *Map of Belknap County*.
32. The level-top stone wall along the spillway, which probably supported the mill building, is fifty-three feet long. As saw logs could be no more than half the length of a sawmill in order to transit the saw, the maximum length of beams from this mill probably would have been twenty-five feet.

CHAPTER 8

33. Vaughan, *Illustrated Laconian*.
34. Hurd, *History of Merrimack and Belknap Counties*.
35. Vaughan, *Illustrated Laconian*.
36. Ibid.
37. Rollins, "Meredith Center"; Woodford, *Map of Belknap County*.
38. Hurd, *History of Merrimack and Belknap Counties*.
39. Based on deeds in the Belknap County Registry.
40. Woodford, *Map of Belknap County*.
41. Maloon, "Glancing Over Meredith's Past."

CHAPTER 9

42. Johnson, *This Grand and Magnificent Place*.
43. Lane, *New Hampshire's First Tourists*.

CHAPTER 10

44. Benton and Barry, *Statistical View of the Number of Sheep*.
45. Vermont Historical Society, "Era of Great Change."

CHAPTER 11

46. Mead, *Up-Country Line*; Lindsell, *Rail Lines of Northern New England*.
47. Blaisdell, *Three Centuries on Winnipesaukee*.
48. New Hampshire Board of Railroad Commissioners.

CHAPTER 12

49. Garvin and Garvin, *On the Road North of Boston*.
50. Wyatt, *Some Meredith History*.
51. Edgerly, *He Did It*.
52. Ibid.
53. Pickering, *Hermit of Meredith Hill*; Robinson, "Joseph Plummer"; Wyatt and Wyatt, *Way Out There*.
54. Maloon, "Glancing Over Meredith's Past."
55. Rollins, "Meredith Center."
56. Sanborn, "Barn Door Sketches."

CHAPTER 13

57. Blaisdell, *Meredith Parade*.
58. Vittum, "Of the Early Bands of Meredith."
59. Ibid.

CHAPTER 14

60. Bear Island Conservation Association, *Bear Island Reflections*; Briggs, *Meredith Neck*; Rollins, *Tourists' Guide-Book*.
61. Bear Island Conservation Association, *Bear Island Reflections*.

CHAPTER 15

62. VanVeghten, *Filling the Void*.
63. Mitchell, *Horse & Buggy Age*.

Chapter 16

64. United States Postal Service, *United States Postal Service.*
65. Ibid.
66. Halfmann, *Clothespins and Calendars.*
67. Rice, *Bob Fogg and New Hampshire's Golden Age.*

Chapter 17

68. Wyatt, *Early New England Farming.*
69. Ibid.
70. Ibid.
71. Wyatt, *Panfull of Knotholes.*
72. Ibid.
73. Ibid.
74. Ibid.
75. Ibid.

Chapter 18

76. New Hampshire Board of Agriculture report, 1905.
77. Curren, *Old Home Day in New Hampshire.*
78. New Hampshire Board of Agriculture report, 1904.
79. Essay and poem by Mary Clough Poore, reported in the *Meredith News*, August 25, 1926.

Chapter 19

80. Bear Island Conservation Association, *Bear Island Reflections.*
81. Carley, *Squam.*

CHAPTER 21

82. Bear Island Conservation Association, *Bear Island Reflections.*
83. Wyatt, *Some Meredith History*.

CHAPTER 22

84. New Hampshire Board of Agriculture, *New Hampshire Farms*.
85. Wyatt, *Some Meredith History*.
86. Quoted in the *Meredith News.*
87. Hosiery boards were used to hold stockings during one part of the manufacturing process.
88. Hardon, "Meredith."
89. Lunt and Lunt, "Prescott Lumber and Meredith."

Bibliography

Adney, Edwin Tappan, and Howard I. Chapelle. *The Bark Canoes and Skin Boats of North America.* Washington, D.C.: Smithsonian Institution Press, 1964.

Bear Island Conservation Association. *Bear Island Reflections.* 2nd ed. Lake Winnipesaukee, NH: Vicks Lithograph, Printer, 2000.

Benton, C., and S.F. Barry. *A Statistical View of the Number of Sheep in the Several Towns and Counties in…New Hampshire.* Cambridge, MA: Folsom, Wells and Thurston, 1837.

Blaisdell, Carl F. *Meredith Parade.* Meredith, NH: Meredith Historical Society, n.d.

Blaisdell, Paul H. *Three Centuries on Winnipesaukee.* Somersworth, NH: New Hampshire Publishing Company, 1975.

Boisvert, Richard A. "Decline of the Ice Age and Arrival of Paleoindians in the Northern White Mountains: The People of the Land." *Windswept* 43, no. 1 (2002).

Briggs, Thomas H. *Meredith Neck.* Meredith, NH: Meredith Historical Society, 1957.

Caduto, Michael J. *A Time Before New Hampshire.* Hanover, NH: University Press of New England, 2003.

Carley, Rachel. *Squam.* Holderness, NH: Squam Lakes Association, 2004.

Curren, Thomas. *Old Home Day in New Hampshire, 1899–1998.* Concord, NH: Inherit New Hampshire, 1998.

Dorion, Christopher. "Decline of the Ice Age and Arrival of Paleoindians in the Northern White Mountains: Part 2." *Windswept* 41, no. 2 (2000).

Edgerly, Asa S. *He Did It, or The Life of a New England Boy.* San Francisco, CA: H.S. Crocker Company, 1909.

Ford, Lena Smith. *Colonial Ebenezer Smith.* Meredith, NH: Meredith Historical Society, n.d.

Garvin, Donna Belle, and James L. Garvin. *On the Road North of Boston.* Hanover, NH: University Press of New England, 1988.

Halfmann, Eunice K. *Clothespins and Calendars: Recollections of the Past.* Canaan, NH: Phoenix Publishing, 1985.

Hardon, Charles. "Meredith: The Gem of the New Hampshire Lakes Region." *Granite Monthly* 9 (1914).

Heald, Bruce D. *New Hampshire Learnin' Days: Dudley Leavitt, "Master."* Meredith, NH: Heald Enterprises, 1987.

———. *Reminisce the Valley.* Weirs Beach, NH: Weirs Publishing Company, 1992.

Hurd, D. Hamilton. *History of Merrimack and Belknap Counties, New Hampshire.* Philadelphia, PA: J.W. Lewis & Company, 1885.

Johnson, Christopher. *This Grand and Magnificent Place: The Wilderness Heritage of the White Mountains.* Durham: University of New Hampshire Press, 2006.

King, Thomas Starr. *The White Hills: Their Legends, Landscape, and Poetry.* Boston: Crosby, Nichols and Company, 1860.

Lane, Charles S. *New Hampshire's First Tourists in the Lakes and Mountains.* Meredith, NH: Old Print Barn, 1993.

Lindsell, Robert M. *The Rail Lines of Northern New England.* Pepperell, MA: Branch Line Press, 2000.

Lunt, Margaret, and Gilman Lunt. "Prescott Lumber and Meredith." *Reminiscences of Meredith: From the 1976 Bicentennial.* Meredith, NH: Meredith Historical Society, 1976.

Lyford, James Otis. *History of the Town of Canterbury, New Hampshire.* Vol. 1. Concord, NH: Rumford Press, 1912.

Maloon, Edgar H. "Glancing Over Meredith's Past." *Meredith News*, December 13 and November 29, 1922.

Mead, Edgar T. *The Up-Country Line: Boston, Concord & Montreal RR.* Brattleboro, VT: Stephen Green Press, 1975.

Meredith Historical Society. *Early Meredith.* Meredith, NH: self-published, 1968.

Merrill, Georgia Drew, ed. *History of Carroll County, New Hampshire.* Boston: W.A. Fergusson & Company, 1889.

Mitchell, Edwin V. *The Horse & Buggy Age in New England.* Ann Arbor, MI: Gryphon Books, 1937.

New Hampshire Board of Agriculture. *New Hampshire Farms for Summer Homes.* Concord, NH: self-published, 1913.

New Hampshire Board of Railroad Commissioners. *Annual Report.* Concord, NH: self-published, 1901.

Parks, Roger N. "New England Textile Mill Villages in the Early 19th Century." Research paper, Old Sturbridge Village, 1967.

Pickering, Agnes N. *The Hermit of Meredith Hill.* Meredith, NH: Meredith Historical Society, n.d.

———. "Meredith School History." *Early Meredith.* Meredith, NH: Meredith Historical Society, 1968.

Potter, Jane S. "New Hampshire's Landscape and Environment." *New Hampshire Archeologist* 33–34, no. 1 (1994).

Rice, Jane. *Bob Fogg and New Hampshire's Golden Age of Aviation.* Portsmouth, NH: Peter E. Randall, 2012.

Robinson, Weld. "Joseph Plummer, The Hermit," *Early Meredith.* Meredith, NH: Meredith Historical Society, 1968.

Rollins, Frank W. *Tourists' Guide-Book to the State of New Hampshire.* Concord, NH: Rumford Press, 1902.

Rollins, Maude W. "Meredith Center." *Old Meredith and Vicinity*. Laconia, NH: Mary Butler Chapter, Daughters of the American Revolution, 1926.

Sanborn, Fred W. "Barn Door Sketches." *Norway Advertiser*, 1916.

Scheiber, Harry N. "Coach, Wagon, and Motor-Truck Manufacture, 1813–1928: The Abbot-Downing Company of Concord." *Historical New Hampshire* 65, no. 1 (2011).

Starbuck, David R. *The Archeology of New Hampshire.* Hanover, NH: University of New Hampshire Press, 2006.

Thompson, Woodrow. "Decline of the Ice Age and Arrival of Paleoindians in the Northern White Mountains: Part 1." *Windswept* 41, no. 1 (2000).

United States Postal Service. *The United States Postal Service: An American History, 1775–2006.* Washington, D.C.: self-published, 2007.

Vadeboncoeur, M., S. Hamburg, C. Cogbill and W. Sugimura. "A Comparison of Presettlement and Modern Forest Composition Along an Elevation Gradient in Central New Hampshire." *Canadian Journal of Forest Research* 42 (2011): 190–202.

VanVeghten, Rudy. *Filling the Void: History of the Meredith Public Library.* Meredith, NH: Meredith Press, 1989.

Vaughan, Charles W. *The Illustrated Laconian.* Laconia, NH: Louis B. Martin, 1899.

Vermont Historical Society. "An Era of Great Change: William Jarvis and the Merino Sheep Craze." Museum and website exhibit, 2004.

Vittum, David A. "Of the Early Bands of Meredith." *Meredith News*, 1928. Series of articles.

Wilcomb, Edgar H. "Meredith's Old Almanac Maker." *Granite Monthly* (n.d.).

Woodford, E.M. *Map of Belknap County*. Philadelphia, PA: Smith & Peavey, 1859.

Wyatt, Esther C. *A Panfull of Knotholes.* Meredith, NH: Meredith Historical Society, 2003.

Wyatt, Esther C., and Harold G. Wyatt. *Way Out There: Chemung & the West End of Meredith.* Meredith, NH: Meredith Historical Society, 1999.

Wyatt, Harold G. *Early New England Farming: Tools and Techniques*. Meredith, NH: Meredith Historical Society, 1999.

———. *Road Histories of Meredith, N.H.* Meredith, NH: Meredith Historical Society, 2004.

———. *Some Meredith History.* Meredith, NH: Meredith Historical Society, 1994.

About the Author

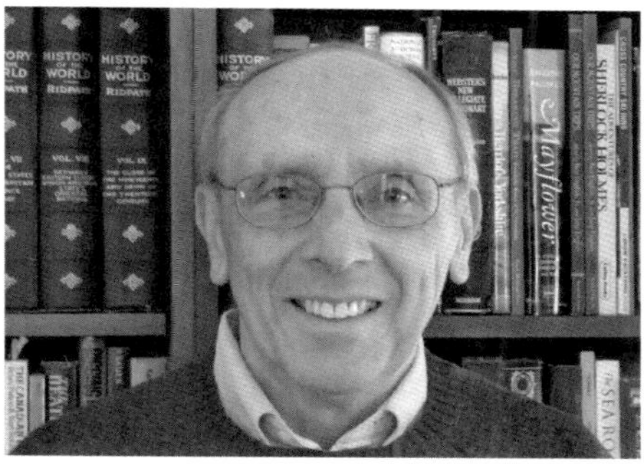

Daniel Heyduk, PhD, has always been interested in people and places. He lived with and studied Nahuatl-speaking people in Mexico and Quechua-speaking people in Bolivia. He did archaeological work on prehistoric hunters in Ecuador and was a college professor of anthropology and prehistory in Maine. While based in New York City, he designed and operated scholarship, fellowship and training programs around the world. Dan now lives in Meredith, in the Lakes Region of New Hampshire, where he is researching and writing about local history. His history column, "Passing Time," appears in the *Meredith News*.

Visit us at
www.historypress.net

This title is also available as an e-book